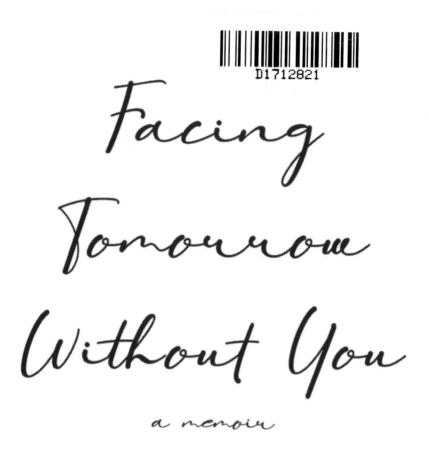

Facing Tomorrow Without You

a memoir

ANNELIESE DALABA

"A beautifully written, faith-inspiring, hope-filled account of one woman's journey with God as she works through grief. After it moves you to tears, you too will be convinced, it should be a must-read for any Christian dealing with loss."

Craig P. Wagner, Ph.D., Psy.D., FIPA
Psychologist and Psychoanalyst

"Grief is so very personal and yet everyone experiences it during their lifetime. The floods of emotions that one goes through are sometimes hard to put into words. Anneliese, in her book, *Facing Tomorrow Without You*, is able to express those emotions so profoundly. Having recently lost my husband of over 40 years, reading this book has enabled me to realize that I am not alone in my grief and that through my grief, God is ever closer to me. Thank you, Anneliese, for putting into words what so many cannot but also experience."

Rev. Sherry Sabella
AGWM Area Director, Southeast Europe

"I have known Curt and Anneliese Dalaba for decades. Their marriage was one of the strongest relationships I know, and she is very transparent in sharing her grief journey with us. Every person deals with grief in somewhat the same manner but also in a unique way as well. The insights into her journey will be a help to those who are currently in the midst of grieving as well as a resource to help in the future."

Rev. Jeff Hlavin
Former Superintendent, Michigan Ministry Network

"Anneliese has created a beautiful tribute to her husband's memory while presenting a valuable gift to the reader. Her skill of intertwining her emotions, Curt's prose, and God's Word offers a blended healing balm that will touch any grieving soul. No matter what loss we may experience, Anneliese shares hope for the future and healing for the heart."

Rev. Mary Selzer
Author, Bible Teacher, and Professional Leadership Coach

"'Sometimes life is just hard … very, very hard!' As a recent widower, this quote from *Facing Tomorrow Without You* summarizes my own journey through grief. Anneliese Dalaba has proven to be a worthy guide leading me along this awful path! Her practical and spiritual insights are invaluable in bringing me back to faith. Her resounding resolve became my own: '… in all things, trust God!' A must read for anyone who has experienced the death of a loved one!"

Dr. David Stair
Professor Emeritus, Evangel University, Springfield, Missouri

"Anneliese Dalaba's book, *Facing Tomorrow Without You*, is a must read for everyone who faces the devastation of living life without those they love. She knows all too well what it means to face the worst, to hurt more than she thought was possible, and how to heal. This book is packed with hope and healing for you!"

Rev. Kevin Berry
Lead Pastor, Mount Hope Church, Lansing, Michigan

"You cannot understand the debilitating grief and loneliness of losing a loved one until it happens. Anneliese Dalaba lost her husband and became familiar with the reality of a broken heart, shattered dreams, and an important decision: Turn her eyes to Jesus and trust His promises … or sink into the raw emotions that now gripped her future. This book is a must-read for anyone who needs an inspiringly honest story of finding peace in the storm of heartache. It may not seem like it, but there is hope."

Rev. Kamron Oberlin
Lead Pastor, Greater Lansing First, East Lansing, Michigan

Facing Tomorrow Without You

Vellichor Publishing LLC
DeWitt, Michigan 48820
www.anneliesedalaba.com
Copyright © 2023 Anneliese Dalaba

ISBN: 9798394379901

Printed in the United States of America.

10 9 8 7 6 5 4 3 2 1

Curt W. Dalaba
July 23, 1955 – September 25, 2020

Dedicated in loving memory
to my dear husband of 33 years,
Curt W. Dalaba

Curt was a credential holder in the Assemblies of God for 42 years (1978–2020) and an ordained minister in the Assemblies of God for 36 of those years (1984–2020). He served as a Michigan Ministry Network official, lead pastor, missionary, associate pastor, and children's pastor during his years of ministry.

His life impacted people from many countries as he served in the United States and abroad. His life touched all age groups and people from various cultures. Curt spoke fluent English, German, and American Sign Language. He dabbled in French, Spanish, and Farsi to communicate with people in his international church and when traveling and ministering overseas.

Curt enjoyed learning about new cultures and customs. He could easily engage with anyone from anywhere and get them laughing with him. His sense of humor, wisdom, and compassion are legendary.

Curt is the father of Amanda (Alireza) Ghanbarpour and Brendon (Kelsey) Dalaba. He was the best dad two kids could have ever wished for. At the time of his passing, he had three grandchildren, Brayden and Lukas Dalaba and Leila Ghanbarpour.

His godly example, integrity, humor, insatiable desire to keep learning, and sense of adventure filled our lives with laughter, education, exploration, and spiritual depth. Curt packed a lot of life and love into his 65 years and left behind an incredible and unforgettable legacy.

Table of Contents

Foreword

Gut-wrenching! An honest expression of feelings! A palpable tension between faith and reality! *Facing Tomorrow Without You* is an intimately personal account of a grieving widow who reflects on the journey of dealing with the untimely death of a beloved spouse.

Getting a grip on grief while hanging on to hope, Anneliese works through a myriad of emotions, processing questions of faith, future, and memories fueled in part by her husband, Curt's, journals and poetry. My wife and I have known the Dalabas for decades as friends and colleagues and shared a small part of her journey after Curt's death.

Anneliese deals forthrightly with spiritual and moral issues and does not conceal the battle of her faith behind the brutal reality of death. Because she and her husband were deeply committed to their faith in Christ, the question of why he died when retirement was near plays a pivotal role in this book. Why wasn't he healed when they, in faith, believed in a God who heals? Why weren't the cancer symptoms manifested and treated sooner? Why did death occur so quickly after the diagnosis? Why couldn't they have had a bit longer with each other, their children, and their three grandchildren?

This account will be a balm for those who face questions of a loved one's death and grapple with grief and life afterward. Anneliese honors her husband and his memory, overcomes the apparent defeat of death with the hope of heaven, and provides a window into the ultimate victory of surrendering to a loving, caring, and encouraging God and His lordship over her life. You will cry, take a deep breath on occasion, smile, and be grateful she recorded her journey for posterity.

Greg Mundis, D.Min.
Executive Director
Assemblies of God World Missions

Preface

After the shock of grief wore off, intense pain and hopelessness overwhelmed me. My only relief came from drawing close to God and being completely honest with Him.

Since I'm a writer, writing was a good way for me to process my thoughts and emotions after my terrible loss, so I chose to blog about my grief journey and the things God was teaching me. I posted on my website once a month the first year after I lost my husband and then occasionally in the second and third years.

Right from the start, I received encouraging comments from readers. Several asked if I'd consider putting my blog into a book format so they could easily reread the content, as well as share it with family and friends. That is how this book came to fruition. It is not word for word as my blog posts first appeared. I took time to add more content and personal stories, but I didn't change the lessons I learned or the order in which I received them.

As you read through *Facing Tomorrow Without You*, you will see it is not in chronological order. That's because we don't go through grief in a specific sequence. Memories come randomly into our thoughts, and feelings are all over the place. You might feel as though you've already dealt with something once and should be done with it, only to have it reappear—

perhaps a bit differently but still the same issue—and you have to process it once more. I have left the chapters in the order that I wrote them on my blog.

My prayer is that as you read this book, you will feel less alone and find hope and strength for your journey. Most of all, I pray that my words will cause you to fall more deeply in love with our Lord and Savior. Truly, no one can comfort us like Jesus.

He comforts us
in all our troubles
so that we can comfort others.
When they are troubled,
we will be able to give them
the same comfort God has given us.
2 Corinthians 1:4 NLT

Introduction

I am not entirely sure where to begin this brief note. I laughed. I cried. In beautifully recounting her own grief journey, Anneliese Dalaba has so vividly described ours that I was taken back in surprise. She writes with such transparency about the life-jarring experience of becoming a widow and her honest grappling with her new reality that one cannot help but be drawn completely into her story. I wish I didn't, but I understand grief. We lost our son at the age of twenty-two to diabetes. I could feel her pain, confusion, and sorrow as I took in each page. As I read her sailboat illustration of death aloud to my wife, Trina, we both wept with joy and sorrow. Grief is like that – one moment life almost seems normal and the next you find yourself sobbing.

What makes *Facing Tomorrow Without You* a must-read is the clarity with which Anneliese simplifies complex theological ideas into simple, concrete facts of life bursting with hope. Hope. Hope right in the fat middle of the grief journey. Throughout her story, she continually calls us back to Jesus, to the gospel, to the hope that He so freely gives us, and that she lives moment-by-moment.

She delightfully weaves her story of growing through grief with poems and journal entries from her husband, Curt. It's as though they wrote this book together. Curt was my friend. I always admired him, but reading Anneliese's book has not only brought healing to this grieving daddy's heart, given me deeper perspective on my journey, but it has also given me an intimate, rare look into the life of a friend that I did not previously have. Reading about how Curt lived, loved, and died makes me want to be more like Jesus.

Thank you, Anneliese, for charting your journey for the rest of us. Your book is a treasure. Your written words will doubtless bring hope and healing to many, and I for one am profoundly grateful.

Rev. Steve Pennington, Ph.D.
Vice Chancellor
Pan-Africa Theological Seminary, Lomé, Togo

Jesus replied,

"You don't understand now what I am doing,

but someday you will."

John 13:7 NLT

CHAPTER ONE

From Laughter to Tears

When our three-year-old grandson, Brayden, walked into our dining room wearing a new t-shirt with the words *Big Brother*, it took only a few seconds for the news to sink in. We jumped from our chairs to hug him and his parents in the midst of laughter and congratulations. Our family was growing, and life was good.

A couple of weeks later, we received a video call from our daughter and son-in-law. They announced that they were expecting their first child. We could hardly contain our joy. In seven months, our family would grow from one grandchild to three!

Everyone planned to come home for Christmas. Joyful anticipation made the task of baking, cooking, and decorating light work. Our daughter and daughter-in-law would be in their third trimester by then.

As Christmas in 2019 approached, the house was beautifully decorated, and in the evenings, Curt and I often sat in the living room and chatted about our day while we dreamed about our future. He was less than a year from retirement, and I would no longer have to share him with a full-time job. We could finally pursue our dreams together, side by side.

The kids soon arrived, and we celebrated a festive Christmas with our growing family. We laughed as we opened gifts. Even the unborn grandchildren received presents.

In the middle of January 2020, our second grandson was born, and in early February, our first granddaughter. We were beyond elated. God had blessed us with two healthy grandbabies.

In March, the COVID pandemic rocked our nation, and we had to quarantine in our homes. While many suffered and people feared losing their health and businesses, Curt and I enjoyed time together at home. He worked in his home office, and I worked in mine, but we met together for breakfast, lunch, and dinner. Every evening seemed like a date night.

We went for walks and talked with neighbors. A new camaraderie developed in our neighborhood. One neighbor put out a portable fire pit as adults and children on our road gathered around to chat.

As the weather continued to warm into May, we spent more time in the fresh air and sunshine and enjoyed talking with other people who had left their houses also in search of some community. But mostly, we enjoyed our time together, just the two of us.

One day toward the end of May, Curt stooped down by the grill, but when he tried to stand, he couldn't put weight on one of his legs. I imagined he had pulled a muscle.

With COVID, it was more difficult to get in to see a doctor and get tested, but after seeing his primary care physician, as well as an orthopedic surgeon, and after several scans and x-rays, we found out at the end of June we were dealing with cancer.

After more scans and an evaluation by an oncologist at the University of Michigan, Curt was diagnosed in July with stage 4 metastatic chondrosarcoma, a very rare bone cancer. The oncologist told us, "At best, with powerful chemotherapy, you may have one to three years to live." They also informed us that Curt needed urgent surgery to place a rod in his leg to help stabilize it since the tumor had eaten away most of the bone and it could break at any moment. They warned that a break would be extremely painful. The oncologist explained all the side effects of chemotherapy, especially since they would have to bring out the big guns to fight this. We understood there was a chance that chemotherapy would not work on this particular cancer.

Curt agreed to the surgery, and it was scheduled for the following week. Could we protect his leg well enough so it wouldn't break while we waited? The surgeon warned us that our local hospital wouldn't have anyone trained to help Curt in such an event. It would require specialized surgery. University of Michigan Hospital was the closest medical facility that would be capable of helping him. Unfortunately, it was an hour and a half away from where we lived. Most insurances would not pay for an ambulance from Lansing to Ann Arbor where the hospital was located. Needless to say, we prayed fervently that his leg wouldn't break in the meantime.

A cloud of heaviness settled over us on our drive home from that appointment. I forced my emotions aside and focused on the task of getting Curt through this. I told him I would support him in whatever decision he made. If he didn't want to do chemotherapy, I would understand.

He thought about it for a moment, then said he wanted to fight the cancer. If it would give him one to three more years, he would have the extra time with our family and especially our grandchildren. There was also the hope that researchers might come up with a new experimental drug in the meantime or God would do a miracle.

How often had we heard testimonies of people who had been given a death sentence of one to three more years, but then God intervened, and they lived for ten, twenty, or thirty more years? Surely, God would do that for us too. We clung to hope like a drowning person to a floating device.

The first week in August, a port was placed for the infusions, and two days later, a rod was placed in Curt's leg. Praise God, it never broke, although his surgeon told us it had been practically hanging by a thread. Once his leg was stable, hope was restored. Curt was out of the wheelchair and moving around with a walker.

However, we didn't know at that time, this would be the last good news we would receive.

On September 25, 2020, Curt took his final breath and entered eternity.

I stared down at my husband's lifeless body. He was gone. If I threw myself on top of him and clung to him, what would be the sense in that? He wasn't there.

I wanted to remember the warmth of the hand I had held only moments before the life-altering words, "He's gone." Everything within me resisted touching his body in case I would feel him grow cold. I didn't want that memory to haunt me. So, I stared down at the shell that was left behind. It had contained the man I loved for over thirty-three years. His body lay still. No movement. The breath of life had vanished.

4

I stood in the palliative care room at the University of Michigan Hospital with my son and daughter beside me—the last room we would occupy as a complete family, the original four. We were no longer complete. One of us was missing.

I felt numb.

I believe numbness from the shock of loss is a gift from God. It worked like a drug to keep me from feeling the depth of my loss while planning a funeral, visiting with friends and family, and making endless decisions. I vaguely remember being amazed at my fortitude. Why wasn't I falling apart? How was it possible that I functioned in many ways as before? No doubt, there were hundreds of prayers for our family, which made all the difference. I found I had the strength I needed to get through those early days of loss.

No Right Time

They said this day was coming,
I prepared as best I could,
To still my lonesome heart from drumming,
And act as others thought I should.

And yet no time seems the right time,
when it's time to say good-bye.

You filled my life in many ways,
I know there'll be an empty place.
No matter how I fill my days,
Still thoughts of you will leave their trace.

For no time seems the right time,
when it's time to say good-bye.

I would have gladly kept you with me,
On this earth for all my days,

And yet I saw how hard it would be,
For you to linger in this haze.

And still no time seems the right time,
when it's time to say good-bye.

To bid farewell, I know I must,
And how it grieves me so,
But now I have a consolation,
That in His arms you safely go.

Though no time seems the right time,
when it's time to say good-bye.
— Curt Dalaba © October 13, 2003

My grief journey had begun. It didn't matter that I wasn't ready. It didn't matter that there were things I still wished to do with Curt or say to him. He was gone. Ripped away. And I had been plunged into the deepest valley imaginable, but the shock of loss continued to hover around me like a thick fog.

I did the only thing I knew to do; I clung to my faith. How often had I read, "God is our refuge and strength, an ever-present help in trouble," (Psalm 46:1 NIV)? He had been my refuge in the past. Surely, He would help me again, but I couldn't imagine how.

My future seemed beyond comprehension. I focused all my attention on God, my only source of hope. I'm sure the enemy, Satan, hoped this would cause me to become bitter, but I called out to God hoping, trusting He would help me. In faith, I said in my heart, "Do not gloat over me, my enemy! . . . Though I sit in darkness, the LORD will be my light." (Micah 7:8 NIV)

God hadn't lightened my darkness yet, but I knew His Word. If I stayed close to Him, surely His light would eventually break through the darkness of my grief.

CHAPTER TWO

God Stayed

I was told that I would be in shock for, at least, the first
month of my grief journey. I didn't understand what
that meant until the end of October. The depth of pain
and loss I fell into at that point is hard to put into
words. Never in my life had I experienced such
hopelessness.

The emotions of grief are varied—actually, all over
the place. One moment I was gripped with a feeling of
unreality, like this couldn't really have happened.
Certainly, Curt would come home soon from a trip. It
was unfathomable that he wasn't coming back to me.
When I looked at his pictures, he was as real to me as
he'd been earlier that year before we even knew about

the cancer.

Then a sense of guilt overtook me. This must somehow be my fault. I should have seen the signs. He complained sometimes that his leg bothered him when we walked too fast during our exercise together. Why did we think it was just that his muscles needed strengthening or he needed to stretch before he walked? Why did we feel no urgency to get it looked at? But would it have made a difference? Not even the big guns of chemo were able to fight off this rare bone cancer.

Of course, God could have stopped it, but for some unknown reason, He didn't. "A person's days are determined; you have decreed the number of his months and have set limits he cannot exceed." (Job 14:5 NIV)

Grief causes one to feel anger. Thankfully, this was the least frequent emotion for me. But there was one moment in December. It didn't last long. I can still see where I stood when I suddenly felt angry at God.

I knew there was nothing too difficult for Him. He could have healed Curt or caused his body to have purged itself from all cancer cells. As I stood staring into my refrigerator for something to eat that afternoon, I was overcome with anger and yelled, "Why did You let this happen? You could have healed him! Why didn't You?" That's about how long my anger lasted.

The truth gripped me and wouldn't let go. God's ways are higher than mine (Isaiah 55:9). God doesn't always interfere in the natural course of life. Since He allowed Curt's life on Earth to end, I must trust Him and believe that it is best for me. That was about the hardest thing to accept. How could that possibly be true?

I don't know the answer to that question. But what I do know is God will never leave me or forsake me (Hebrews 13:5). And that quickly, my emotions changed again, and I entered into praise. It was a sacrifice of praise. Nothing had changed. But in faith, I believed God would see me through this and even cause good to come out of it.

In December, over two months after I lost Curt, I walked into my living room where my Christmas tree was set up. This room had been Curt's favorite during the Christmas season. It was homey and cheerful. We would each sit in one of the upholstered chairs and talk about our day or the kids or our plans or whatever came to mind. It was a sweet way to end the day in our cozy cocoon apart from the rest of the world. It was "our" time, and we treasured it.

How much had changed from the year prior when we anticipated the joy of two more grandchildren joining our family. There was laughter, hope for the future, and Christmas cheer all around.

Now I stood alone in that room. His chair sat empty. I fell to my knees, overwhelmed with longing and sorrow, and sobbed uncontrollably. The one person who could comfort me best was the very person I was grieving.

But eventually the tears subsided, and my heart lifted with thanksgiving to God for the beautiful memories. I had found a treasure many will never find. I had found my true love, my soulmate, my closest friend, my spiritual leader, and so much more. I was blessed by God to spend thirty-three years of my life with such a man—my husband—who loved me completely, as Christ loves the Church.

I had to ask myself the question Job asked, "Shall we actually accept good from God but not accept adversity?" (Job 2:10 NASB) Has God changed because He allowed cancer to take Curt from me? No. He was absolutely the same loving Father He always had been.

Many years ago, Curt and I, along with his parents, visited the Adirondack Mountains in New York where my father-in-law owns five acres of land. We hiked up

11

to his property, and my father-in-law gave us a tour. Eventually we arrived at a huge boulder. He pointed to a large indentation on the side of the rock where a person could crouch and find protection from a storm. He called it a cleft in the rock. It reminded me of the song by Fanny Crosby.

> He hideth my soul in the cleft of the rock
> that shadows a dry, thirsty land.
> He hideth my life in the depths of his love,
> and covers me there with his hand,
> and covers me there with his hand. [1]

I needed God's protection now. I needed Him like never before in this darkest of valleys, alone, without my husband and dearest friend. I felt vulnerable and needed God to hide me in the cleft of the rock and cover me with His hand.

Curt was gone now, but God was still here with me. For some unfathomable reason, He allowed this to happen. I couldn't see His plan for me, but I knew my God. As I submitted to Him—even while my heart was heavy and I cried tears of sorrow—I knew God would help me, and somehow, He would be glorified through my terrible loss and through my life. Something good would come out of it. In faith, I chose to trust Him.

> I will hide beneath the shadow of your wings
> until the danger passes by.
> I cry out to God Most High,
> to God who will fulfill his purpose for me.
> My heart is confident in you, O God;
> my heart is confident.
> No wonder I can sing your praises!
> For your unfailing love is as high as the heavens.
> Your faithfulness reaches to the clouds.

Be exalted, O God, above the highest heavens.
May your glory shine over all the earth.
(Psalm 57:1–2, 7, 10–11 NLT)

[1]. Fanny Crosby, He Hideth My Soul, 1890, Public Domain

CHAPTER THREE

Faith and Tears

The loss of a husband is so much more than just losing a marriage partner. To show what I mean, I'll have to share some of my memories of Curt.

We were married about a year when I became pregnant with our first baby. Before I had a chance to bond with the life growing inside of me, I miscarried. The hardest part about this loss was that Curt was leaving on a trip to Pakistan at the same time, and if he didn't make it home safely, I wouldn't have his baby to give me comfort—to have a part of him to hold onto. Thankfully, Curt arrived home, and I conceived again. I had an ultrasound before the sex of the baby was recognizable. Curt thought our baby looked like a lima bean (one of his favorite vegetables, by the way), and he began to refer to our baby as LB. We laughed about it. He had such a great sense of humor, something I treasured about him. But once we found out it was a girl and gave her a name, he didn't call her that anymore.

Amanda was born one month prematurely and only weighed 5 pounds, 3.5 ounces. Although we had to face the very likely possibility of losing her soon after birth, Curt and I leaned on each other. We were partners in this crisis. And thank God, we were able to share in the joy of answered prayers. Amanda survived neonatal respiratory distress syndrome and pulmonary hypertension. Her quick recovery surprised the doctors and nurses. As Amanda gained strength, she became a very good eater, and by the time she was a little more than two months old, she weighed 10 pounds. She had round, rosy cheeks and a double chin. At that point, Curt said she reminded him of Winston Churchill, and he would talk to her in a similar voice as Winston Churchill. It was hilarious.

When our son and daughter were in their early teens, we spent a family vacation on gorgeous Nantucket Island. While Amanda and I took a bus to go shopping downtown, Curt and Brendon rented mopeds to explore the island. It was the first time Brendon had driven his own moped. Curt wanted to do something his son would enjoy and always remember, and he provided well for Amanda and me so we could enjoy a fun shopping trip at the quaint shops on the island. We have many fun memories of vacations with our children.

Curt and I traveled to various countries. I've not taken the time to count them, but my favorite place of all was Grindelwald in Switzerland. He took me there on our honeymoon, then again with our small children and his parents, and finally for our thirtieth wedding anniversary.

Curt knew how much I loved that charming, little village in the canton of Berne situated in the Alps. It is 3,392 feet (1,032 m) above sea level. While there, we took a ski lift to the top of Grindelwald–First Mountain (7,165 ft or 2,184 m), which is known as a cable car station above Grindelwald. The high elevation on that mountain makes it difficult for vegetation to grow on parts of it. You can see clouds when you look down and you can walk through snow even in the summer. The panoramic view of snow-covered mountain peaks, blue sky above, and mountain villages as you look down is breathtaking. I thought that spot must be the closest thing to heaven here on Earth. I will always think of Curt when I think of Grindelwald.

On another trip, we took a sky ride up a mountain in Vorarlberg, Austria. After hiking around the top, we decided to walk down the mountain. I'm so glad we did. There was beauty all around us—things we would have missed if we had taken the sky ride instead.

I loved Curt's enjoyment of exploration. One summer, he and I spontaneously decided to pack our bags, along with a book of Michigan lighthouses. The kids were mostly independent now and would be fine without us for a week, so we took off in our car to explore as many Michigan lighthouses as we could in a few days. We hadn't booked any hotel rooms to stay in. We'd do that at the end of each day when we got tired of driving. This turned out to be one of our favorite vacations. We snapped pictures as we hiked through woods and over dunes. We laughed and shared conversation the entire way up the west coast of Michigan and into the Upper Peninsula.

These precious memories of Curt illustrate how much is lost when you lose your spouse. I'll share just one more. This is probably one of the things my children and I miss most about him. He was our encourager. He always inspired us to use our gifts and pursue our dreams.

When I wrote my first novel, I had several family members cheering me on, but no one could out-cheer Curt. And I don't think there was anyone prouder about my accomplishment. Almost immediately, he began asking me about my next novel. He closely listened as I laid out the plot. His words of affirmation strengthened my fingers to fly over the keyboard on my laptop.

When I received a book award in Florida in November 2019, I can still see Curt in the audience taking pictures, a broad smile lighting his face. I'm certain Curt never read a romance novel in his life except my first two books.

He would have read my third novel too, if he'd lived long enough for it to have been published. Around June of 2020, as we waited for a diagnosis about his leg, I read to him the first chapter of my third book. Again, he entered into the story and laughed at just the right places. Curt was a far more gifted person than I am, but he always made me feel like I was the one who was special and fascinating.

The memories of him seem endless. When you lose a husband, you lose far more than a spouse. A marriage partner isn't the only thing I lost. No, I lost exponentially more.

- father of my children
- grandfather of my grandchildren
- someone to cuddle with and keep me warm
- best friend
- confidante
- defender/protector
- prayer partner
- pastor
- Bible teacher

- someone to dream with
- provider
- travel companion and travel guide
- mower of our lawn
- snow removal person
- handyman
- comforter
- encourager
- driving partner
- date
- comedian (He was the best at making us all laugh and finding humor in things.)
- walking encyclopedia (The man knew so much!)
- theologian
- German-speaking partner (We often conversed in German.)
- etc.

No one has time to sit and read about all the things I lost when Curt passed away. I'm sure I could continue adding to the list all day long and shed a thousand tears. The loss is mine, and I must bear it. Strangely, it's part of my loving Father's plan for me.

"You keep track of all my sorrows. You have collected all my tears in your bottle. You have recorded each one in your book." (Psalm 56:8 NLT)

> So it is only for a little while that God takes from us our loved ones. We shall have them back again, made into immortal beauty. The hopes we mourn as having perished, are yet in Christ's hands. He will keep them safe for us and at length will give them back to us in radiant and imperishable loveliness. ... One of the surprises of heaven will be our finding there the precious hopes, joys, and dreams which seemed to have perished on earth—not left

behind—but all carried forward and ready to be given into our hands the moment we get home.

—J.R. Miller [1]

How beautiful heaven will be. No more heartache or tears. No more diseases or death. No more goodbyes. Instead, a happy reunion awaits us. And best of all, we will finally look into the eyes of the One who loves us most of all. Come, Lord Jesus. Please come soon and carry us home.

Oh, I want to see Him, look upon His face,
There to sing forever of His saving grace;
On the streets of glory let me lift my voice,
Cares all past, home at last, ever to rejoice.

— R.H. Cornelius [2]

"He will wipe every tear from their eyes, and there will be no more death or sorrow or crying or pain. All these things are gone forever." (Revelation 21:4 NIV)

[1]. J.R. Miller, Love In Taking Away, The Ministry of Comfort, CreateSpace Independent Publishing Platform, 2014, pg. 11

[2]. R.H. Cornelius, Oh, I Want to See Him, 1916, Public Domain

CHAPTER FOUR

Never Alone

Twenty weeks into my grief journey, there were moments when I still felt as though this didn't actually happen. Perhaps I'm stuck inside of a nightmare. Maybe I'll wake up and find Curt beside me, healthy and whole, able to walk, run, and jump. Then reality would sink in, and I experienced my loss all over again. How could this possibly have happened to us?

It's not that I didn't know Curt was gone. I wasn't in denial. I knew what was real and what wasn't. It was just that sometimes when my phone dinged to let me know I had a new text, for just a second, my heart leaped. *Curt's texting me to tell me where he is and when he'll be home.* In the next second, I remembered that was no

21

longer possible, which forced me to accept what I could not change. I had acknowledged the loss, but my subconscious mind had not fully embraced it yet.

I realized it would take time for the truth to settle into the deepest recesses of my mind. Those moments of unreality were less frequent than at the beginning, yet it still happened. And each time I accepted my new reality, it was soon followed by loneliness. The more I understood how permanent my loss was, the bleaker my future on Earth seemed.

At such moments, I needed God to fill the void. Anything else that I could have run to would only have brought temporary relief. Eventually, I would have had to deal with my loss. And if a person runs to the wrong things, they will compound their loss with guilt, regret, shame, or a waste of time. Jesus is the only one we can run to when we need our burdens lifted. And just running to Him once doesn't fix it for all times. I found that many days I ran to Him and filled my mind with His Word several times a day. This reminds me of the famous quote by Corrie Ten Boom: "You may never know that JESUS is all you need, until JESUS is all you have."

In my Griefshare class, they instructed us to be honest about our needs with those closest to us. For example, let people close to you know how to pray for you specifically. The first person that came to mind was my sister. She prays for me all the time. I asked her to please pray that I would have the constant assurance that I'm not alone.

Once I told her, I didn't think about it anymore. I had done what I was supposed to do, so I let it go. That evening, I read a book about heaven and another helpful book about comfort, and then I got ready for bed. The next morning, I awoke with a song on my mind that I probably haven't sung since I was a teenager. There was no reason the words should have been playing in my thoughts, and yet they were.

> When in affliction's valley
> I tread the road of care,
> My Savior helps me carry
> My cross when heavy to bear;
> Though all around me is darkness,
> And earthly joys are flown,
> My Savior whispers His promise:
> "Never to leave me alone."
>
> No, never alone,
> No, never alone;
> He promised never to leave me,
> Never to leave me alone.
>
> He died for me on Calv'ry's mountain,
> For me they pierced His side,
> For me He opened that fountain,
> The crimson, cleansing tide;
> For me He's waiting in glory
> Upon His heavenly throne:
> He promised never to leave me,
> Never to leave me alone. [1]

How thankful I am for God's faithfulness to me. "The LORD is near to all who call on Him, to all who call on Him in truth." (Psalm 145:18 NASB) I cling to this promise, and so can you. Grief comes in many forms, not always the loss of a loved one. People grieve many disappointments in life. We live in a fallen and sinful world, and we aren't immune to how this will affect us. No matter what we face, this promise is a reassurance to us of God's faithful care. If we've placed our trust in Jesus, we are not alone.

[1]. Anonymous, Never Alone, Public Domain

CHAPTER FIVE

The Weight of Grief

On Monday, I had a great day. It felt like the heaviness of grief had lifted. The sun finally broke through the clouds. I almost felt normal again. This reprieve from sadness lasted until Tuesday morning.

But on Tuesday afternoon, the weight returned. It's not easy to describe it to someone who's never gone through this before. We've all felt the burden of disappointment and various kinds of grief, but when you lose one of the most significant people in your life, the burden of grief is unimaginable.

Thank God I have discovered that in this place of utter loneliness and with a heart so heavy it could anchor a ship in deep water, God is nearer still. His

Word encourages my heart. His promises give me hope. His sacrifice assures me that my loss is not permanent.

Whenever Curt and I planned a vacation while our children were little, I would begin talking to my children about all we would do during our time away. As I drove to the store with both children strapped in the back seat of the car, I'd entertain them by going over the details of our vacation plans. When I ran out of things to tell them, my seven-year-old daughter would call from the back, "Mommy, let's talk about vacation again." Their hearts were filled with anticipation, and they wanted to know more. Somehow, hearing about their upcoming vacation gave them a foretaste of the joy that awaited their arrival.

Since Curt passed away, I've been curious to know what he's experiencing in heaven. As one of his close friends told me after Curt's funeral, "Curt already has the answers to our many questions." Faith has become sight. And knowing Curt is there has piqued my interest like never before. I've been reading books about heaven because, just like my children anticipated vacation, I want to know all I can about what awaits me. And what I've learned so far has whet my appetite. I can hardly wait to arrive.

When we were preparing for the mission field, my husband went ahead of us to find a home to rent. He didn't want to arrive there with his family in tow and have no place to live. So, on his own, Curt searched and found a lovely townhouse that fit our budget and our needs. When everything was signed and ready for us to move in, he came back for us. When the kids and I saw our new location and home for the first time, we loved it. Curt had prepared well for our arrival.

In some ways, this is how our separation now feels. It's as though Curt has gone on ahead of us to scout out our new home. I imagine he's seeing and experiencing many things already that he cannot wait to show us.

Knowing Curt, he's looking forward to our arrival with as much joy and anticipation as we feel about seeing him again.

The more I read about heaven, the more I long to enter the place God has prepared for those who love Him. It seems God wants us to feel this way about our eternal home with Him. "Therefore, if you have been raised with Christ, keep seeking the things that are above, where Christ is, seated at the right hand of God. Set your minds on the things that are above, not on the things that are on earth." (Colossians 3:12 NASB)

I have focused so much on heaven that it's created an urgency within my soul to share Jesus with everyone I meet and to do good deeds to those around me. I'm praying for many who are still lost. God loves them and wants them to see the place He has prepared for them and for us. It is more amazing than any vacation anyone has ever taken on this earth. I've seen some majestic scenery in my lifetime. Curt took me to the Alps in Switzerland, Austria, Germany, and Italy. I have seen lakes and oceans that were so crystal clear that we could see to the bottom. I have seen and walked through old castles in Germany, and I have seen modern architectural structures and man-made islands in Dubai in the United Arab Emirates. But not one of these earthly wonders can compare to all that awaits us.

"No eye has seen, no ear has heard, no mind has imagined what God has prepared for those who love Him." (1 Corinthians 2:9 NLT)

CHAPTER SIX

Greater Reality

When Curt began his battle with cancer in the summer of 2020, he posted on Facebook about the greater reality. Here are his words from that post:

> A couple days ago in the morning, while waiting for the results from the nuclear scan, I was reminded of my own sermon on the greater reality (faith). In 2 Kings 6, there's a story about Elisha and his servant. They were surrounded by an enemy army. This army was their reality. Elisha was calm. The servant was a nervous wreck. The difference was that the servant could only focus on the reality, but Elisha was aware of the greater

reality.

Elisha prayed, "Lord, open his eyes to see that there are more with us than there are with them."

On the mountain tops were what Elisha saw: chariots of fire!

So, our reality is a giant named cancer. The greater reality for us is that the Lord is near us, and we hear Him, and we feel hopeful. I pray that God keeps our eyes glued to the mountaintop and not what's coming down the driveway.

After Curt passed away, this post haunted me. I couldn't bring myself to re-read it. We had both hoped and prayed that God would reveal His greater reality to us by overpowering cancer and healing Curt completely. That didn't happen—not here on Earth. It was easier to ignore this post than to reflect on it. But in the back of my mind, I knew I would have to reexamine it one day and discover what God was saying to me.

Curt's Facebook post came to mind again recently. I did a search and found it. As I re-read it, I was surprised that Curt never talked about healing when he spoke about the greater reality. He said, "I pray that God keeps our eyes glued on the mountaintop and not what's coming down the driveway." Had he spoken prophetically? At the time of this post, we didn't even know what type of cancer he had or in which phase it was.

Toward the end of Curt's life, despite the pain he endured and the disappointment of not improving physically, he said with tears in his eyes, "I love God so much." His hope remained in the Lord, the God he'd dedicated his life to serving. And Curt served Him faithfully and with integrity.

It reminded me of what I had read countless times in Hebrews about the faith of Abel, Enoch, Noah, Abraham, and Sarah. They held onto the promises of God in faith.

"All these people died still believing what God had promised them. They did not receive what was promised, but they saw it all from a distance and welcomed it. They agreed that they were foreigners and nomads here on Earth. Obviously, people who say such things are looking forward to a country they can call their own. If they had longed for the country they came from, they could have gone back. But they were looking for a better place, a heavenly homeland. That is why God is not ashamed to be called their God, for he has prepared a city for them." (Hebrews 11:13-16 NLT)

This verse says *they did not receive what was promised*. God's promises to us are not always fulfilled in our lifetime, but that doesn't make them lies. His promises are for all eternity.

The verse goes on to say, *but they saw it all from a distance and welcomed it.* This tells me that they didn't waver in their faith even when it looked like God hadn't kept His promise. They chose to trust and believe anyway because these faith-filled followers of God understood that God's promises are from generation to generation. They do not end. They are eternal.

Curt was a man of multiple talents, interests, and hobbies. He was a phenomenal expository preacher, wise counselor, and leader of men. But he was also gifted in art, photography, poetry and other writings, languages, and much more. Curt was fascinated by life and wanted to explore as much as he could. Yet his life was cut short.

I will not doubt though sorrow falls like rain,
And troubles swarm like bees about a hive.
I believe the heights for which I strive

Are only reached by anguish and by pain;
And though I groan and writhe beneath my
crosses,
I yet shall see through my severest losses,
The greater gain.
— Curt Dalaba

It's tempting to ask God, "How could you take one so educated, wise, and gifted? He still had so much to offer. How much could have been accomplished for the Kingdom if he had lived twenty more years."

But this life is the practice ground for eternity. None of Curt's talents are wasted or lost. His best writings will be in heaven. Every language he learned and every life lesson has prepared him for his responsibilities in the next life. And his joy of exploring and discovering new territory will have no end when Curt sees all God has prepared.

This world is our reality, but the greater reality is that there is more to come.

So, with the Lord's help, I continue to keep my eyes glued to the mountain top, and not on what's coming down the driveway. May this grief journey never be wasted. Instead, may it strengthen my faith, teach me more about God, and prepare me for eternity.

CHAPTER SEVEN

A Bitter Cup

I went for a walk with a friend a few months after my loss. We live in the same town, so we met at a specific spot and enjoyed some time together. It was a nice distraction. Once we parted, I walked the short distance home alone. It was then I realized that the last time I walked on that sidewalk, I had been pushing Curt in his wheelchair. My heart squeezed tight—so many firsts.

Every day I trudge along with homesickness and longing that nothing on this earth can fill. A bitter cup was placed to my lips, and I was forced to drink it. Half of me wished I had died with Curt. But then I would remember my children and grandchildren, God's calling on my life, and I knew my work wasn't finished yet. There were lives I needed to touch and prayers I still had to pray. So I joined my voice to the Apostle Paul's and said, "For to me, to live is Christ, and to die is gain. But I am hard-pressed from both directions, having the desire to depart and be with Christ, for that is very much better; yet to remain on in the flesh is more necessary for your sakes." (Philippians 1:21-23 NASB)

No one understands better what I'm going through than Jesus. Not that I compare my sorrow to His. Not at all. Although blameless, He suffered for my sin. Coming to Earth meant false accusations, hatred, deceptions, and the painful death of a criminal. He did nothing to deserve such shame. Can you imagine how homesick for heaven He must have felt? The price for our salvation was a bitter cup only He could drink.

> The record says He was exceeding sorrowful, even unto death. 'Being in agony, He prayed.' The Holy Sufferer pleaded that the cup of bitter anguish now being held to His lips might pass from Him. Never was more intense prayer offered to the Father. But amid the anguished pleading, was heard the self-restraining word of submission, 'Not My will—but Yours, be done.' There was something more important than the granting of the suppliant's request—it was that the purpose of God for Him that hour should go on unhindered.

> There is no other way by which true comfort can come to any heart in time of sorrow but by acquiescence. So long as we cannot say, 'Not my will—but Yours, be done,' the struggle is still going on, and we are still uncomforted. Comfort is peace, and there is no peace until there is acquiescence in the will of God. Whatever the sorrow, therefore, if we would find divine comfort

—we must seek to bring our will into complete harmony with our Father's will.

—J.R. Miller [1]

I choose to surrender to God's will for me. It's impossible to hide from sorrow, so I embrace the pain and endure it so that I may be healed. At the same time, I'm keeping my eyes on Jesus and reminding myself that He's in control. "And we know that God causes all things to work together for good to those who love God, to those who are called according to His purpose." (Romans 8:28 NLT) Somehow ... someway ... this is all for good in my life. It's hard to fathom it now, but I believe His Word.

I must also keep in mind that when God promises good things to me, I may not see the fulfillment until eternity. This Earth is only temporary, and so is my loss. Eternity will last forever, and we will be reunited there.

Curt wrote a blog post in 2003 called, *Uh, Excuse Me!* With it, he posted a picture of a buffalo standing in the middle of the driving lane, with oncoming traffic on the other side. Its message speaks to me now.

"Sometimes things move slowly. Sometimes they come to a grinding halt. So, how do I make progress with a buffalo in the way? I suppose I could pass the beast. Hmm, on the left that would mean a head-on collision. On the right, a soft shoulder followed by a respite in the ditch. Maybe I should shoot the beast. Uh, no, very illegal. Plus, the thing is cute in an ugly sort of way. I think I'll just stay on track and wait this one out.

"I don't know what buffalo is impeding your progress today. Buffalos take on all shapes and sizes. Don't do anything drastic. Just stay on track.

They do move eventually. You'll get moving again."
— Curt Dalaba

Today, I choose to surrender to God, stay on track, and trust Him.

After Curt's funeral, a friend from church gave me a gold necklace with three letters engraved on it: YES. After opening the gift, I looked at her.

She read the question in my eyes. "It's for the times you don't understand. It's to remind you that you said, 'yes' to trusting God."

I cannot tell you the countless times my hand has reached up to my neck and my thumb caressed the letters on that necklace as tears streamed down my face. I said, "Yes." I meant it. I haven't changed my mind, nor will I.

YES

Yes to all He commands.
Yes to wherever He leads.
Yes to however He expands me.
Yes to every rebuke.
Yes to every new task.
Yes to every surprise.
Yes to every gift He gives.
Yes to every gift I must give.
Yes to every insight.
Yes to every correction.
Yes to whatever He's doing.
Yes to silence.
Yes to jubilant rejoicing.
Yes to subtle speaking.
Yes to clarity's boldness.
Yes to day-by-day plodding.
Yes to miracles.

Yes to challenges.
Yes to servanthood.
Yes to exaltation.
Yes to divine prodding.
Yes to Jesus formed in me.
Yes to my will dying.
Yes to divine compliments.
Yes to divine instruction.
Yes to avenues unknown.
Yes to momentary roadblocks.
Yes to alternatives revealed.
Yes to the unexpected.
Yes to heavenly care.
Yes to heavenly silence.
Yes to humble pleading.
Yes to boldness, claiming.
Yes to old self dying.
Yes to resurrection life.
Yes to others' glory.
Yes to vineyard weeding.
Yes to vineyard sweating.
Yes to vineyard waiting.
Yes to vineyard disappointing.
Yes to joyous vineyard harvesting.
Yes to the Spirit's secret working.
Yes to joy unspeakable.
— Curt Dalaba

Oh, may I always be like Mary, who said "yes" to God even though others would look at her with disapproval or skepticism. She didn't take time to count the cost of her obedience. She didn't ask to sleep on it before she decided. Instead, "Mary said, 'Behold, I am the servant of the Lord; let it be to me according to your word.'" (Luke 1:38 ESV)

I want to submit to God's plan in the same manner as Mary had. It will take time to heal, but I can submit immediately.

I am the servant of the Lord. Let Your will be done.

[1]. J.R. Miller, Comfort in God's Will, Ministry of Comfort, CreateSpace Independent Publishing Platform, 2014, pg. 19

CHAPTER EIGHT

Faith Intensified

There were times I stood by a framed picture of Curt in my family room and talked to him. It seemed to help me to process my grief. Today, I told him that if the Lord should tarry, I will grow old while he will remain the same in all his pictures. Curt was six years older than me, but now he's in a place where time doesn't exist. If the Lord should tarry and grant me good health, I will continue to grow older and eventually age beyond Curt's 65 years at the time of his death.

"Behold, I am telling you a mystery; we will not all sleep, but we will all be changed, in a moment, in the twinkling of an eye, at the last trumpet; for the trumpet will sound, and the dead will be raised imperishable, and we will be changed." (1 Corinthians 15:51–52 NASB)

Woohoo! By the time Curt sees me, I will have shed my aging body and been clothed with an imperishable body.

We speculate and try to understand the afterlife by what we read in Scripture and what we imagine, but no one can fully know all that God has prepared for us. We cannot even fully understand God. There are many unanswered questions.

Here is what Curt wrote about knowing God:

> "Oh, what a wonderful God we have! How great are his riches and wisdom and knowledge! How impossible it is for us to understand his decisions and his methods! For who can know what the Lord is thinking? Who knows enough to be his counselor?" Letter to the Romans, Chapter 11, Verses 33-34.

> I love this God. Although He is a God who reveals Himself, I can't totally figure Him out. Although He is a God of order, I can't systematize Him. He won't let Himself be totally understood, because we humans would try to contain Him and control Him. That's why people often prefer a neatly packaged god or spirituality.

> Is it acceptable to say we don't fully understand Him? Obviously, Paul thought it was because I just quoted Him. I know so much more about this God than I ever did, but I am still learning. I know Him, but I don't. I understand Him, but I don't. I know His ways, but I don't. I like the fact that He's mysterious.

> I know that what I am responsible for, He will

make known. Beyond that, much is tied up in mystery, and I'm okay with that. There's no way I could contain all He knows anyway. Too much knowledge would be overwhelming for me and overbearing to others. I will trust Him to let me know what I need to know, when I need to know it, and in what measured dose I need to receive it.

A few weeks after Curt's funeral, when my family had all returned to their homes, I came downstairs that first morning, and the weight of all I'd lost felt excruciatingly heavy on my shoulders all at once. It was as though a dark, weighted blanket had been thrown over my body and soul. Words fail to adequately describe the hopelessness I felt about never seeing Curt again in this life. Having to learn to live without him thoroughly and completely overwhelmed me.

Curt always said I was an optimist. I lost all optimism that day. Not even a speck remained. Joy had abandoned me. I couldn't imagine ever finding happiness in this life again. The shock of grief had worn off, and I felt the intense depth of my loss.

I struggled along throughout that day, putting one foot in front of the other, taking a breath, and then another breath, and then another. The day finally ended, only to fall asleep and have to do it all over again the next day.

But God stayed beside me, and my understanding of Him expanded. He revealed Himself to me in the measure that I needed Him. Praying and reading my Bible helped. Reading books about heaven and grief helped. Talking to family and friends helped. Messaging and emailing with friends helped. Exercising helped. Helping others helped me too. Before I knew it, I reached the five-and-a-half-month mark since Curt left, and I realized that joy *was* returning.

Do I still miss him? Yes! Every day. I can't make it

through a day without tears. Nevertheless, God is healing me as He comforts me day by day.

This poem Curt wrote describes well the process of my grief journey. The memories that hurt and delight. The faith that arose when my frozen emotions burst free of the shock that had helped me endure the first part of grief. When I began to feel the extent of my loss, faith intensified. As I gazed toward my Savior, the hope of eternity beckoned like never before.

The Day I Laid You Down

Many roads we've walked together,
I, scarce, begin to count them all,
At times my mind is overwhelmed,
With all the memories I recall.

You are the salt, did not Christ say,
You added flavor to all my days,
You are the light, did not He say,
You helped to brighten my dreary ways.

With you, I've oft been moved to laughter,
With you, at times, yes, moved to tears,
With you, our joys to highest rafter,
With you, together, moved through fears.

But no day had moved me deeper than the day I laid you down.

I lay you down, seed sown in spring,
I walk away with cherished hope.
That one sweet day new my life will bring,
With this thought only do I cope.

I have left you, not alone,
But in the soil of God,

And holding steadfast to his promise,
I move on, this life to trod.

With great delight, anticipation,
One day again to you I'll cling,
For now my greatest aspiration,
Is the joy that he will bring.

For no day will thrill me stronger than the day you
take your crown.
— Curt Dalaba ©2002

CHAPTER NINE

God Sees and Provides

Of all the emotions of grief, sadness has been my constant for months, and unreality likes to visit often. But as I mentioned before, I've recently had days where I almost feel normal. Ironically, as soon as I realize I'm having a good day, the tears return. It seems wrong to have a good day when Curt is still missing from my life. He deserves, at least, a year of constant tears. I know how ridiculous that sounds but knowing it in my head is not the same as feeling it in my heart.

Curt would be the first to tell me it's okay to cry, and it's okay to feel normal. He would encourage me to allow my heart to heal. To embrace the good days and thank God for them because bad days will soon follow.

That's just how it is when grieving someone who meant the world to you. So, I'm learning to enjoy the respite and keep on living.

Last weekend, my three-year-old grandson and I had 24 hours together, just the two of us. My day was full of activities—even my grand-nephew joined us for several hours. Now that Opa—that's German for grandpa—doesn't need his side of the bed any longer, my grandson was only too happy to share the bed with me. He went to bed early, so I did too—because that's what an Oma does when her grandchild doesn't want to be alone. When Brayden left the next day, I waved goodbye from my window.

My home felt empty. It's a familiar feeling now whenever the kids and grandkids depart. Curt used to take me into his arms at this point, and we would share the empty feeling—and soon, we enjoyed just the two of us again. Now, the emptiness lingers. I fill it with busyness, but it creeps back again.

That night as I lay in bed, memories of Curt's struggle with cancer plagued my mind. I told myself, "It's over. He's healed now." And I prayed. Soon I fell asleep and began to dream.

I arrived in heaven. Curt stood off at a distance with his arms wide open and a big smile spread across his face. I ran toward him and threw myself into his embrace. He held me so tight that my feet lifted off the ground and he spun me around. We clung to each other and laughed. I cannot begin to describe the joy I felt. All the heaviness had melted away. My heart was full. I was whole again.

Then I awoke. Instead of being disappointed that it had only been a dream, joy lingered even in my wakefulness. I whispered, "Thank you, God. I needed that dream."

He whispered into my heart, "I will provide everything you need."

"You thrill me, Lord, with all you have done for me! I sing for joy because of what you have done. O Lord, what great works you do! And how deep are your thoughts." (Psalm 92:4–5 NLT)

Oh, the wonder of the love of God. He sees into the deepest part of my soul. He knows the longings I cannot express. He sees the need even before I sense it. He strengthens. He fills. He restores. He heals. God works patiently and lovingly, step by step.

Ever Present, Here Again

You are here again,
Unending cycles of a cycleless God.

Ever-present God,
Showing himself again.

The God who never leaves,
Arrives at my doorstep again.

Solid tree ever present,
Bursts forth in new leaves.

River ever present,
With new water constant flows.

Overshadowing God,
Blows fresh wind to clear my day.

The great Almighty,
Approaches me as a gentle Lamb.
— Curt Dalaba ©2005

CHAPTER TEN

Living While Grieving

In September of 1987, we became one when we married. In September of 2020, we were wrenched apart through death. Thirty-three years of partnering together in life, loving and assisting each other. Facing every high and low of life together. Is it any wonder I feel as though I've undergone an amputation? No longer a whole person. Half of me is missing.

That's how I felt as I sat alone at the gate waiting for my first flight as a widow. Single again. Curt wasn't there to listen for the call to board. I had to look out for myself. He was no longer there for me to talk to or reminisce with. I looked at all those around me. Everyone a stranger. It was no different than the many times Curt and I had traveled together, except we had each other then. Come what may, we were together. Whenever our eyes met in a crowded airport, a warmth of familiarity and intimacy enveloped us. Now I stood alone ... and, oh, the loneliness.

"Have mercy on me, O God, have mercy! I look to you for protection. I will hide beneath the shadow of your wings until this violent storm is past. I cry out to God Most High, to God who will fulfill his purpose for me. He will send help from heaven to save me ... My God will send forth his unfailing love and faithfulness." (Psalm 57:1-3 NLT)

I am reminded that I'm not alone. When the pain of my "emotional amputation" becomes too great, God reminds me that He is with me. It's not an empty promise. As I turn my thoughts toward Him, I begin to see life from the perspective of eternity. Real-life will start when we reach the next life. We are in a vapor right now, but there is so much more that awaits us. This earth is temporary. Most things we experience here won't last beyond death. My grief won't last forever either.

But I'm still on this earth, and right now, grief is painful. I need God's help to get through it, so I cling to the promises in Scripture. "The LORD himself goes before you and will be with you; he will never leave you nor forsake you. Do not be afraid; do not be discouraged." (Deuteronomy 31:8 NIV)

So when my heart hurts, as it often does, I purpose to set my eyes on Him again. Practicing this is increasing my understanding of who He is and all He can provide for me if I will allow it.

Yes, I do allow it. I long for Him. He isn't just my better half—He's my everything.

"We give attention to our grief today, but we ask for your help to redirect that attention to the hope

that we have in the resurrection of Jesus Christ. It's hard to say goodbye because that was never your original intention. We were not created for separation, and this is our struggle. But you have come that we might have life. You are greater than our grief. Today we are sad, but soon we will be glad, as our hope overshadows the sting of death."
— Curt Dalaba

"The Lord's unfailing love surrounds the one who trusts in him." (Psalm 32:10 NIV)

Yesterday, a motorcyclist revved his engine outside the open window of my daughter and son-in-law's apartment. My one-year-old granddaughter ran to me and looked wide-eyed toward the window, clearly afraid of the noise. I lifted her into my arms, and she snuggled against my chest, placing her soft curls beneath my chin. No tears escaped. She was safe. And I enjoyed her trust. Eventually, the noise faded away, and she got down on the floor to play again.

Oh, how the Lord is pleased when we trust Him like that. In His arms, striving ceases, and I surrender my will.

Will my soul ever cease to praise?
My heart its banner ever raise?
God, the center of devotion
Inhabiting every single motion
Of faith-filled hearts aglow
Yearning always just to know ...
The gaze of His great love.
— Curt Dalaba ©2005

CHAPTER ELEVEN

Sometimes We Wait

It's disconcerting to read a passage in the Bible that appears false. I never encountered this dilemma until after my husband died. It baffled me. Certainly, the Bible is *always* right. I'd heard that all my life. But now some verses felt like unfulfilled promises.

For example, "And we know that in all things God works for the good of those who love him, who have been called according to his purpose." (Romans 8:28 NIV) I had believed every word of that verse. But what about now? Curt loved God and so did I. So, why did God allow cancer to take him from his family and ministry? How was that for anyone's good?

Getting angry at God wasn't the answer for me.

That's not how I react to frustrations. Instead, I want to fix the problem or research about it and find answers. Anger feels like a waste of time. I'd rather take action. So, I forced myself to take a closer look at that verse and several others.

I continued to read the Bible and I prayed for Biblical discernment. After all, the Holy Spirit is the best Bible teacher.

Here was my dilemma: 1) God's Word is always true; 2) How can this verse be true when what I lost is irreplaceable?

If a parent loses a child, how can this verse still apply to their lives? Even if they gained ten more children, not one of them could replace what was lost. The wound may heal, but the scar would still hurt whenever it's bumped. If a husband loses his wife and remarries, one wife cannot replace another wife. He may love his new wife, but I imagine he will continue to miss his first wife. She was such a big part of his life and heart. Beautiful memories will always awaken loss.

Everything within me wanted to scream, "How is this good?"

We read in the Old Testament about Job's terrible loss. I'm glad God restored his losses. Everything, except his children. Oh, Job had more sons and daughters, but the ones he had lost were gone forever and irreplaceable. So, I imagine Job could never feel the depth of joy he had before his loss. He would always miss them.

One of the things Curt taught me was how to interpret the Bible more accurately. For years, we pastored an international church. We lived in a university town, so those who attended our services came from all over the globe—twenty-eight to thirty different countries were represented. No separate services for different language groups. We believed that our church should look a lot like heaven, where we all worship together in one accord. We also lived and ministered for several years in Germany among refugees. Working with internationals forced us to broaden our perspective of God and the Bible.

If our interpretation of Scripture only applies to a few, then we are wrong. In other words, if how we interpret a Bible verse only applies to middle-class or wealthy Americans, but not to the homeless or those living in war-torn countries, then our interpretation of Scripture is shallow and incorrect.

Back to Romans 8:28. It's hard to accept this verse at first glance when believers in Jesus Christ come to the end of their lives and some of their prayers weren't answered. Despite their love for God, they didn't see all things work together for good in their lives. Does that mean God's Word isn't true?

Of course not. What it means is our interpretation is incorrect. I'm certainly not a Bible scholar or theologian, but I realized God never claimed this life was all there is. There are countless blessings we won't reap until we reach eternity. But eternity lasts a lot longer than an earthly lifespan. I'd rather receive my greatest blessings where time never ends.

"'The Son of Man must suffer many things and be rejected by the elders and chief priests and scribes, and be killed and be raised on the third day.' And He was saying to them all, 'If anyone wants to come after Me, he must deny himself, take up his cross daily, and follow Me. For whoever wants to save his life will lose it, but whoever loses his life for My sake, this is the one who will save it. For what good does it do a person if he gains the whole world, but loses or forfeits himself?'" (Luke 9:22–25 NASB)

Jesus's life on Earth was not an easy one. He had enemies who followed him around and even infiltrated his close-knit group of friends. Jesus knew they were there, but it didn't deter him from obeying the Father.

In the end, he was falsely accused by one of his followers, condemned to die, and his death was excruciating.

So I must ask myself a hard question … and so must you. But the answer to that question will determine our attitude when we face disappointment, heartbreak, disease, lost dreams, violence, etc. When things are at their worst, am I still willing to trust God?

"These things I have spoken to you so that in Me you may have peace. In the world you have tribulation, but take courage; I have overcome the world." (John 16:33 NASB)

Jesus told us that we would face tribulation in this life. He never promised it would be easy. Only by casting our cares on Him does our burden become lighter. If the worst happens but you choose to trust God, He is faithful to help you carry the load. Jesus never said that there would be *no* burden. What He said was, as we cast our cares on Him, our burden would become light, and we would find rest.

"Come to Me, all who are weary and burdened, and I will give you rest. Take My yoke upon you and learn from Me, for I am gentle and humble in heart, and you will find rest for your souls. For My yoke is comfortable, and My burden is light." (Matthew 11:28–30 NASB)

Sometimes we experience blessings on Earth. I've certainly had my share of blessings in this life. It almost didn't seem fair at times that I should be so happy and content while others suffered. I savored those blissful moments and praised God. They were gifts that I never took for granted.

But now that God, in His unfathomable love, knowledge, compassion, and benevolence, allowed me to lose one of my most cherished blessings, would I continue to trust Him and even praise Him? Would I still believe God "causes all things to work together for good to those who love God, to those who are called according to His purpose"? Did you notice it says, *His* purpose—not my own. He knows what's best. God's plans are for all eternity.

"And all these, having gained approval through their faith, did not receive what was promised, because God had provided something better for us, so that apart from us they would not be made perfect. Therefore, since we also have such a great cloud of witnesses surrounding us, let's rid ourselves of every obstacle and the sin which so easily entangles us, and let's run with endurance the race that is set before us, looking only at Jesus, the originator and perfecter of the faith, who for the joy set before Him endured the cross, despising the shame, and has sat down at the right hand of the throne of God." (Hebrews 11:39-40 and 12:1-2 NASB)

Like Abraham, Sarah, Moses, Gideon, Rahab, Samuel, and so many others who walked this life before us, are we willing to endure the cross and continue to trust God that all things will work together for good even if we do not receive everything we pray for in our lifetime? Are you okay with receiving the answer to your prayer or your reward in eternity and not on Earth if that is what the Lord requires of you?

That was the question staring me in the face after I lost Curt. As tears streamed down my face, I said, "Yes." And then I asked the Lord to come back soon. Today or tomorrow would be great. Let's get this suffering over with and be done with it.

But what if God makes me wait? What if I have many more years with this homesickness and longing for what I have lost? Will I keep my eyes on the promise?

I would hate to have to wait that long, but, yes, even then, Jesus. Even then, I will continue to trust You as You give me grace and strength to do so. I cast my cares on You because You care for me (1 Peter 5:7).

* * * *

Ambassadors of Truth

If you truly represent his kingdom,
you will be a light in dark places.
Keep burning brightly.

If you truly represent his kingdom,
you will be a pure stream flowing into a muddy
river.
Don't get absorbed.

If you truly represent his kingdom,
you will speak the truth when the world screams
louder.
Keep talking.

If you truly represent his kingdom,
you will not always be understood.
Know him and understand yourself.

If you truly represent his kingdom,
you will find contentment amidst a very
discontented people.
Keep smiling.
— Curt Dalaba ©2005

CHAPTER TWELVE

Grieving With Eternity in View

My children and I stood together as the nurse bent over Curt. She lifted her head, her gaze met ours, and she softly spoke, "He's gone." Two simple words, but their impact was indescribable. A life well-lived that filled our world, directed our lives, embraced, provided, comforted, and loved us so well, now gone. Snuffed out. How many nights did those two words echo in my mind as I tried to fall asleep? I cannot tell you.

I came across a short story that helped take away the sting of those final words.

I'm standing upon the seashore.
A ship at my side spreads her white sails to the

morning breeze,
and starts for the blue ocean.
She's an object of beauty and strength,
and I stand and watch her until, at length,
she hangs like a speck of white cloud
just where the sea and the sky come down and
mingle with each other.

Then, someone at my side says, "There! She's gone!"
Gone where? Gone from my sight—that is all.
She is just as large in mast and hull and spar
as she was when she left my side,
and just as able to bear her load of living freight
to the place of destination.
Her diminished size is in me and not in her.

And just at the moment
when someone at my side says, "There! She's gone!"
there are other eyes watching her coming;
and other voices ready to take up the glad shout:
"Here she comes!"

And that is dying. [1]

    I could easily picture this illustration of a sailboat in my mind. My family immigrated to the US from Brazil when I was seven years old. My grandmother sometimes came to visit us, and she would stay for a year or several years. Then, she'd fly back to Brazil again to be with her other children and grandchildren. Every time she left, we cried. She had become such a big part of our lives, and it hurt to see her go.

    But as we waved a tearful goodbye, our family in Brazil leaped with joy at my grandmother's arrival.

    Reading the story above, I pictured that hospital scene once more. I heard the words, "He's gone." But this time it didn't end there. Instead, in my mind, I saw the many who preceded Curt—his grandparents, his uncles, his aunts, my grandparents, and many he ministered to until they took their final breath—now standing and shouting, "Here he comes!"

I love thinking about heaven, where I will one day be reunited with Curt. Looking forward to that reunion doesn't diminish my joy of seeing Jesus, my Lord. It doesn't take anything away from my worship of God. It only enhances my praise because, without Christ, a reunion would be impossible. I imagine that on the day Curt and I throw our arms around each other, we will lift our voices in joyous praise to God who made it all possible. He will be at the center of our joy—always and forever!

The Folded Tent

And so it's been from the beginning, life has been so good to me.
Oh the beauty I enjoy, oh the family and the friends
On this journey in God's bright and blessed world I roam,
I can't imagine this could ever end.
One more road to travel, one more song to sing,
It seems my tent has just unfolded, as I take a look around.

The winds have blown, the rain has fallen,
Threatening storms have filled my site,
I held down fast this little, small one,
So much to see, so much to do, so much wonder yet to live.
Storm, you shall not take it; I'll hold tight.
My tent's not ready to be folded; it's not time to lay it down.

I gather you about me, for I long to see your face,
There's one more thing I've got to say,
Before I leave this place,
I've cherished you in living, oh I cherish you in
death,
For loving is a pleasant way,
To draw one's final breath,
For I see my tent is folding and I'll have to lay it
down.

Of late I've found a strange new drawing,
To another place so fair,
I hear His voice, to me is calling,
To a place where there's no care.
So I've let go, released my soul and bid farewell,
And now my tent has folded and it's time to lay it
down.
— Curt Dalaba ©2004

"I have fought the good fight, I have finished the
race, I have kept the faith. Now there is in store for me
the crown of righteousness, which the Lord, the
righteous Judge, will award to me on that day—and not
only to me, but also to all who have longed for his
appearing." (2 Timothy 4:7–8 NIV)

[1]. Luther F. Beecher (1813-1903), Gone
From Sight, (Often attributed to Henry Van Dyke)

CHAPTER THIRTEEN

Grieving With Hope

Joy is finally returning, yet I realize it's not the joy I once knew. No matter the beauty or pleasure of the moment, an undercurrent of sadness—a void—remains. Deep joy seems impossible since I lost Curt. I can smile and laugh. I can enjoy so much of life. But the sheer, gray veil of grief before my eyes stays firmly in place. If the grandkids do something adorable or reach a new milestone, I long to look into Curt's eyes and share a moment of pride and pleasure. When I'm with my family and we laugh together about something, I miss hearing Curt's laughter joining ours. It's like I'm living life in a haze of sadness. Everything would be more fun if Curt were here.

I spent last week in Pennsylvania with my sister and brother-in-law. My brother joined me for the trip. On Sunday, we planned to attend my brother-in-law's church before my brother drove us back to Michigan where we live. My sister planned to join us so she could visit our Michigan family.

It happened to be the seven-month anniversary of Curt's passing. I had experienced two good days before Sunday. But that morning, realizing which day it was, I could feel the weight of grief once again. I wiped away tears through most of the worship songs at church but did fine through the rest of the service. As we prepared to leave, I told my sister and brother that I wanted to sit in the back seat of the car and work on my computer. I had writing projects that needed my attention and distracting myself helped to temporarily lift the heaviness of grief. This worked well while driving through Pennsylvania and Ohio.

When we got into Michigan, onto Route 23 North, nothing could stop the terrible sadness from returning. I tried reading, listening to an audiobook, talking to my brother and sister, but nothing helped. We would soon be driving on the part of 23 near the University of Michigan where Curt had spent his final days on Earth. I had driven my car on that road to home and back to the hospital many times while Curt was undergoing treatments. Everything within me rebelled at the thought of being on that highway. It hurt too much to remember. If only I could forget.

> Unless the Lord had helped me,
> I would soon have settled in the silence of the grave.
> I cried out, "I am slipping!"
> but your unfailing love, O Lord, supported me.
> When doubts filled my mind,
> your comfort gave me renewed hope and cheer.

But the Lord is my fortress;
my God is the mighty rock where I hide.
(Psalm 94:12-15, 22 NLT)

In my desperation, I looked up at the night sky from the back window of my car and prayed, *God, you know how much I miss Curt. But I trust you. I trust you completely, my Lord.*

The weight lifted. It doesn't happen that fast every time, but it did on Sunday. I lay my head on the back of my seat, put in my earphones, and was able to concentrate as I listened to a book with my eyes shut.

I'm so thankful for my brother and sister who understood my need for seclusion most of that day. Grief is strange that way. Sometimes the last thing I want is to be alone. Other times, I long for solitude. It's wonderful when friends and family try to understand and give the grieving person the freedom to choose.

It's amazing how reaffirming my trust in God helps to lift me up. It was probably about two months into my grief journey that I began to understand how much it pleases God when His children choose to trust Him, especially in the most difficult or disappointing circumstances. It's easy to say we trust God when everything is going well. But it's another thing to trust Him when your world has fallen apart.

The Bible says that God is the same yesterday, today, and forever. If He was trustworthy when all was going well, then He is still trustworthy when things fall apart. That means I can trust Him no matter what my circumstances may be. He hasn't changed. And when I grasp this and start praising God and placing my complete trust in Him, the burden becomes lighter. It's not something I do once, and the grief is gone. No. I must come back to the same point over and over again. It still takes time to heal. I still cry. But I no longer feel quite as hopeless when I remind myself that I trust God with my future and even with my unanswered questions. God's presence helps to lift the burden for a while so it's not as heavy as it had been.

> There is a void inside my heart
> An empty spot no one can fill
> I lost someone I dearly loved
> And wish that they were with me still.
>
> I have my moments when I think
> This subtle ache will never leave
> That grieving could go on so long
> Without some comfort to receive.
>
> I reached for something, someone near
> To understand what I must feel
> But no one knows how much you meant
> To me to give a word to heal.
>
> Words when spoken often fail me
> If comfort they could, I'm sure they would
> Yet only the psalmist understood
> The nearness of God is my good.
> — Curt Dalaba ©2006

CHAPTER FOURTEEN

How Will I Respond?

I was offered a writing assignment with a tight deadline seven months after losing my husband. The following month, almost all my waking hours were spent on that project. Being super busy helped to distract me from my grief, yet at times it still broke through. When you miss your spouse or another loved one who was crucial to your happiness and enjoyment of life, the pain of that loss bursts through every attempt at distraction. I soon realized I was better off if I embraced the pain when it came, allowed myself to feel it intensely, told God about it, cried my eyes out, and gave God the opportunity to comfort me. When I did that, the heaviness lifted, and I was able to move forward with my life, until the next wave of grief hit.

Some people find great comfort in listening to music, especially worship songs with words that encourage. I was one of the ones who had a hard time listening to music the first three or four months after my loss. Music made me sadder and caused unbearable pain. I prayed. I read the Bible, books on grief, and especially books about heaven. I listened to sermons about the end times. I so wanted the rapture to happen so I could leave here, and my family and I could be with Curt again. Selfish, I know. But the hope of heaven and finally seeing God's plans for this earth move toward the grand finale gave me something to anticipate with joy. But then I remembered that God's delay in returning is because He still wants more people to turn to Him and repent of their sins.

"The Lord is not slow in keeping his promise, as some understand slowness. Instead, he is patient with you, not wanting anyone to perish, but everyone to come to repentance." (2 Peter 3:9 NIV)

My children, grandchildren, and I went to the Adirondack Mountains in upstate New York for my husband's graveside service in May, eight months after his passing. Curt's parents and sister met us there. One of Curt's cousins did the committal service.

It was painful to see my husband's name on a tombstone with a birth date followed by a date of death. It's one of those moments that leaves you staring and shaking your head in disbelief. How did something that seemed impossible to imagine happen so soon?

There were flashes of memories almost too difficult to bear. Curt getting the news from his doctor over the telephone that he had metastatic, stage-4 cancer. Sitting in the oncologist's office and hearing him tell us that, at best, Curt would have one to three more years if the chemo worked. Hearing a hospital physician tell me there is nothing more they can do. "Call your children to come today if they want to see their father while he can still hear them." Looking over at Curt after that bit of news, I asked him, "Did you hear?" He slept so much that I wasn't certain he'd been awake. The look of sadness on his face as he gave a brief nod will stay with me forever. He was both heartbroken and resigned.

As heart-wrenching as those moments were, I loved him so much that I'm glad I could be there with him. I cherished each moment we still had.

One of the days after we realized we were dealing with the type of cancer that had a hopeless prognosis outside of a miracle from God, Curt and I sat together on the front porch of our home. Every task that needed doing seemed insignificant compared to our need to be together. We talked, but I don't remember what we said. I only remember wanting to savor his nearness. Because if God in His sovereignty chose not to heal him, I would soon be sitting on that front porch alone.

Months later, after planting flowers in my garden, I sat on the porch chair Curt had sat on that day. That memory flashed before my eyes. I was alone now. I couldn't stop the tears.

Sometimes life is just hard—very, very hard. But how will I respond in those moments? Will I cling to the faith I claimed to have, or was it all lip service while everything was going my way? Gut-wrenching moments are opportunities for faith to rise and give us hope for the future. The reason we can have hope is that God is still with us. He didn't go away when our loved one passed over to eternity. God is still near.

In Acts 28:3-6 NIV, we read: "Paul gathered a pile of brushwood, and as he put it on the fire, a viper, driven out by the heat, fastened itself on his hand. When the islanders saw the snake hanging from his hand, they said to each other, 'This man must be a murderer; for though he escaped from the sea, the goddess Justice has not allowed him to live.' But Paul shook the snake off into the fire and suffered no ill effects. The people expected him to swell up or suddenly fall dead; but after waiting a long time and seeing nothing unusual happen to him, they changed their minds and said he was a god."

Grief can be like that snake. We ask God, "Why?" Over and over again. It's tempting to be mad at God because He had the power to spare me this grief, but He refused. It would be so easy for me to stay focused on my broken heart. But if I do that for too long, my heart might become bitter. I must shake off the temptation to point my finger at God the same way Paul shook off that snake. In God's wisdom, He chose to take Curt home.

The truth is, God loves Curt, and God loves me. Since He allowed me to suffer this loss, there is a reason why this was better for us even though it broke our hearts into a thousand pieces. Am I willing to trust God? As I said previously, God is more interested in our happiness for all eternity than on this earth. Eternity will last forever. So am I willing to trust Him with my future by accepting His sovereign plan in my life on Earth, which the Bible describes as a vapor, here today and gone tomorrow?

I want to share with you something my husband wrote in his journal several years ago. He based this on Acts 28:3-6, which I quoted above.

We spend way too much time examining the vipers that attach themselves to us. Vipers are poisonous and must be dealt with promptly. Do not examine the viper, do not fear what is going to happen if the venom enters your veins. Get rid of the thing.

When temptation comes, when anxieties increase, when confusion prevails, SHAKE IT OFF. Get rid of the thing. Examine and study later. But action is what you need at this point. Vipers may even be beautiful, but they are deadly. Shake them off.

It wasn't even Paul's fault. The viper was there. The heat of the fire, the circumstance of the moment brought it to the surface. Paul did not waste time in examination. He acted straightaway. Study how to avoid vipers later; act now.
— Curt Dalaba

I don't want to allow the temptation to distrust God to seep into my heart. I refuse to doubt His ability or willingness to heal. I will not question God's love for me. Instead, I choose to cling to faith. I will keep reminding myself that there are so many others who seemingly never received that for which they'd hoped.

Hebrews 11:13 NIV says, "All these people were still living by faith when they died. They did not receive the things promised; they only saw them and welcomed them from a distance, admitting that they were foreigners and strangers on Earth."

We aren't home yet. We are foreigners and strangers here. One day all the promises God gave to us will be fulfilled, but perhaps not in this life. Perhaps not until eternity. Am I willing to accept that?

Yes, I choose to accept God's will. But acceptance of God's sovereignty does not mean my pain will disappear immediately. God's Word in Hebrews 13:5 NIV is what I cling to, "Never will I leave you; never will I forsake you."

Anteroom: Faith & Hope

One tries to reconcile himself to a place
that has caused him greatest pain
yet holds the potential of his greatest

joy in working. At times the memory
of what has transpired outweighs
the hope of what can happen but
has not yet happened—the desire
to bring closure—close the door
on a painful yesterday while
waiting in the anteroom to
tomorrow's joy—in this
waiting room, one looks for
escape—yet not through the
door of tomorrow's joy—escaping
yesterday without embracing
tomorrow—destroying this
anteroom destroys this only
door to joy—a joy connected
to yesterday's sorrow, a
sorrow never bathed in hope,
never drenched with redemption,
a wasted sorrow, a seed
without fruit—a travailing
womb that bears no child
but as one gropes through dim
light for the knob that opens
the door, hope is its only
inner compass, faith its only
fuel. When faith wanes the
room spins, and hope cannot
find its way—the room
between yesterday and tomorrow
is called today, which can
only be navigated through hope
and faith.
— Curt Dalaba ©2020

During the first week after Curt passed away, my
son said to me, "I don't want to waste my grief. I want
to learn all I can from it, and I want to grow. Dad's

death will not have been in vain in my life. Whatever I must learn, I want to learn it well."

He spoke the words that I felt in my heart also. I will not waste my grief. The only way I can gain the most from my loss is by trusting God and disciplining myself to submit to Him. He wants to comfort me, and He knows just how to do it. I choose to trust Him.

CHAPTER FIFTEEN

The Precious Gift of Grief

I pulled weeds yesterday evening from a flower bed that I used to admire without having to do much of the work. Curt was the gardener. Working in the garden was therapeutic for him. While I did the housework inside, Curt spent time in the yard. When he finished, he'd call me to come and look at it.

He did such a great job. And I was glad *I* didn't have to do the gardening. I admired the flower beds and trees from the windows of my house throughout the spring, summer, and fall. I loved sitting outside or walking in the backyard and seeing all the plants and flowers blooming.

Last night, however, as I bent over another tall

weed, pulled with all my might, and threw it on the ground to join the others, my back ached from bending over and moisture covered my brow. I straightened and looked toward the deck where I used to stand and tell Curt how beautiful it all was. Oh, how my life has changed. Everything was so much better then.

I glanced down at Curt's gardening gloves on my hands and shook my head. Our dreams for the future looked nothing like this. For years we anticipated and planned for our retirement. It had almost been in our grasp. But without warning, it was snatched away. We were partners for life. Now I stood alone. I no longer loved my life as much as I used to.

This morning I read, "If any of you want to be my follower, you must give up your own way, take up your cross, and follow me. If you try to hang on to your life, you will lose it. But if you give up your life for my sake and for the sake of the Good News, you will save it." (Mark 8:34–35 NLT)

Nowhere in the Bible does it tell me that all my dreams will come true here on Earth. Consider the cross Jesus had to carry for our sake. It was a far more grueling and humbling cross than the one I must bear, but He did it for us. There was no other way to save the world from damnation.

I fully trust that God took Curt home because there was no other way to accomplish His plans for the two of us. What those plans are, I have no idea. But I *do* trust God.

In Hebrews 12:2 NLT, we read this about Jesus: "Because of the joy awaiting him, he endured the cross, disregarding its shame."

Jesus endured the cross by focusing on the joy yet to come. Does that mean that if we honor God by trusting Him when hard times come and accept our cross without griping or angrily lifting a fist at God, that there is an extra reward awaiting us in eternity? I don't know, but I know there will be rewards, and I imagine this might be an opportunity to receive one. What I do know is that Jesus showed us by example how we are to endure our cross.

"He was oppressed and treated harshly, yet he never said a word. He was led like a lamb to the slaughter. And as a sheep is silent before the shearers, he did not open his mouth." (Isaiah 53:7 NLT)

Jesus felt every thorn, whip, spit, tearing out of his beard, and slap. Jesus felt the frustration of false accusations from arrogant and ignorant people. He was not immune to their mockery. He dreaded the unjust ruling by self-serving political leaders. That's why he prayed in Luke 22:42 NLT, "Father, if you are willing, please take this cup of suffering away from me. Yet I want your will to be done, not mine." He was not spared the agony of the nails or the dying of his body. He felt grief for those who wept as they knelt at His feet. Yet He led a sinner (the criminal hanging beside Him) to salvation by His humble example in *how* He endured the cross.

> Take up your cross.
> Your cross is what you take up
> for the good of others. You need
> not like it, not enjoy it—but
> you do enjoy the horizon's promise,
> a promise of new life.
> —— Curt Dalaba

Curt once told me that our cross isn't about what happens to us but what we endure for others. That my husband had cancer and died is not my cross to bear. That happened to me. But facing my loss in such a way that will glorify my Savior and draw people's attention to God, *that* is my cross. It's something that doesn't come naturally, but I must do it for others. That doesn't mean I shouldn't cry. It doesn't mean I can't say that I'm hurting and still in the process of healing. But interestingly enough, I have learned that reaching out and helping others while I'm grieving helps me in my healing process too.

As I stared at all I'd lost, I teetered toward hopelessness. But at that moment, I felt as though God had placed a finger under my chin so I would look into His eyes. By lifting my gaze to Him, He gave me the ability to see those around me who are hurting too.

While Jesus hung on the cross in absolute misery from the horrendous torture He continued to endure, He saw His mother and her intense sorrow. Then He turned His gaze upon John, His disciple, and asked him to take care of her. Although in excruciating pain and dying, Jesus saw Mary's need.

> We should never allow ourselves to face toward life's glooms; we should never sit down in the shadows of any sorrow and let the night darken over us into the gloom of despair; we should turn our face away toward the light and quicken every energy for braver duty and truer, holier service. Grief should always make us better and give us new skill and power; it should make our heart softer, our spirit kindlier, our touch more gentle; it should teach us its holy lessons, and we should learn them, and then go on with sorrow's sacred ordination upon us, to new love and better service. It is thus, too, that lonely hearts find their sweetest, richest comfort.
>
> —J.R. Miller [1]

If you've recently entered your grief journey, it's perfectly normal to feel your loss intensely. You will need time to grieve. How long grief lasts varies between individuals. No one should compare one person to another. But no matter how long it takes, cling tightly to your faith even when you don't understand. Your broken heart makes it possible for you to attain a deeper level of love for your Savior than ever before.

> To fall in love with God is the greatest of all
> romances, to seek Him, the greatest adventure.
> — St. Augustine

Because you need God so desperately right now to comfort you, this is your opportunity to fall deeply in love with Him like never before. That is the one and only precious gift of grief. Just like spouses fall deeper in love when they join together and care for each other through the trials they must face, in the same way, we fall more deeply in love with God when we cling to Him as we take halting steps forward on our grief journey.

In Matthew 14, we find the incredible story of when Peter walked on water. As long as Peter had his eyes on Jesus, he was able to walk on the water. But when he focused on his circumstances, he began to sink. I'm learning this lesson on my grief journey too. If I keep my focus on Jesus, I find it possible to have peace, joy, fulfillment—and most definitely hope. But when I focus on my circumstances, I begin to feel lonely, unhappy, and hopeless.

It's all about perspective. The last couple of years of Curt's life, he preached at many churches about the importance of maintaining a proper perspective on life and in our Christian walk.

Perspective reminds me of the allegorical religious poem, "Footprints in the Sand". When the person in the poem saw only one set of footprints in the most difficult moments of his life, he thought he'd been abandoned. But then he learned that when he only saw one set of footprints, they were not his own but the Master's. In those darkest moments of his life, the Master had carried him. This knowledge changed his perspective and helped him to feel loved, sheltered, and protected. Same circumstances, but a different perspective made all the difference.

There was so much the disciples didn't understand while Jesus walked this earth. Jesus knew this about them, and He was patient with them. I love the story in the Bible when Jesus is transfigured on the mountain while Peter, James, and John watched. Peter makes a very human suggestion that lacks godly wisdom.

The Bible tells us in Mark 9:6 NLT, "He (Peter) said this because he didn't really know what else to say, for they were all terrified."

I've often had a self-deprecating smile on my face as I read this because I understood how Peter must have felt. I hate long moments of silence when with a group of people or even just one person, especially when I don't know them well. If no one else will start a conversation, I feel I must. So when the Bible says that Peter said this because he didn't really know what to say, I understood him. I probably would have said something stupid too and then slapped a hand over my mouth in mortification.

While I was in the deepest point of grief and filled with despair for my future without Curt, I don't remember all I said to God. I'm sure some of it came out of human emotion. But Jesus didn't rebuke Peter, and He didn't rebuke me, either. He did, however, ask me a simple question, "Do you trust me?"

It took me aback. I felt like God had let me down. He allowed my husband to die, and now He asked *me* if I trusted Him. It would seem unreasonable, except I knew that I am blind and ignorant about the future, while God has perfect vision and complete knowledge about tomorrow and every day thereafter, even into all eternity.

I knew God loved me so much that He allowed Himself to suffer and stay on the cross to die for my sins. I knew His plans for my life are always for good. No matter how disappointed I felt, I knew God's character. God is all-knowing, He's always faithful, He only wants what's best for me, and He loves me more than anyone else in this world is capable of loving anyone.

So, my answer to God's question to me was a fervent, "Yes, I will trust You." With those words, my despair went away. I still had to move through my days, weeks, and months of grief, but hope lit the way.

No one knows me as well as God does. He knows the deepest desires of my heart. He knows me better than I know myself. For that reason, I knew He hadn't abandoned me. His plans for my future didn't die with Curt. I believe they are in the process of being fulfilled.

The disciples' perspective had been wrong. They didn't understand that Jesus had to suffer and die so that everyone would have the opportunity to spend eternity with Jesus. They had been hoping for an undefeatable, political leader here on Earth to help them conquer their enemies. Their hopes were for this life here on Earth. They didn't get it until Jesus had ascended into heaven. That's when they finally understood that it's not about the here and now. It's about eternity.

The fulfillment of my dreams is not about this life, either. God is far more interested in fulfilling His plans for me for all eternity.

In the meantime, I cling to the promise Jesus gave to anyone who will trust Him:

"Don't let your hearts be troubled. Trust in God, and trust also in me. There is more than enough room in my Father's home. If this were not so, would I have told you that I am going to prepare a place for you?

When everything is ready, I will come and get you, so that you will always be with me where I am." (John 14:1–3 NLT)

[1]. J.R. Miller, The Duty of Forgetting Sorrow, The Ministry of Comfort, CreateSpace Independent Publishing Platform, 2014, pg 31

CHAPTER SIXTEEN

A Band-Aid for Grief

Nine months into my grief journey, I realized one day that I was tired of grieving. Tired of hurting. It was tempting to try to hide from the pain by filling my time with other things, mind-numbing things, anything to distract my thoughts away from my loss. There are numerous ways a person can avoid dealing with their heartache, but sooner or later, it all comes tumbling back again. You can't hide forever.

For example, my sister and her family live about ten hours from me and came for a visit. My days were full. We talked about Curt sometimes, of course, which brought tears but laughter too when we shared memories of things he said. He had such a great sense of humor. Most of our time together was filled with playing with our grandchildren, feasting, chatting, activities, and catching up on everyone's life. By the time I dropped into bed at the end of each day and listened briefly to an audiobook, I soon enjoyed the oblivion of sleep.

All too quickly, it was time to say goodbye. I braced myself for it hours before they left. I knew what would follow. It's what happened every time I've had to say goodbye to my family now that Curt was gone. After waving and blowing kisses, I entered my house, shut the door, and an avalanche of grief crashed over me. The empty feeling when family leaves now merges with the loss of my husband and is overpowered by that nine-month-old grief, and the pain is re-awakened and overwhelming.

It's tempting to run and hide in a captivating book, a movie, or call my kids and focus on their lives, anything to occupy my mind so that I don't think about loneliness, emptiness, sickness, death, or memories of what can never be again. There is nothing wrong with doing any of the activities I mentioned, except when they are just a Band-Aid on a deep and gaping wound. Insufficient.

After my sister left, I put on my sneakers, clicked the leash on my dog's collar, and went for a long walk. I cried and told God how much I miss Curt, but my heart stayed heavy. Then I remembered what had helped me before. Nine months into the grief journey has taught me some things. I've felt this desperate longing countless times since September 25, and I knew what I needed to do. It was like the Lord whispered into my ear, "Come, spend time with Me. Place your trust in Me again. Praise Me and thank Me for what I'm doing in your life. I still have things I want you to accomplish. I'm preparing you. I'm already using you. Trust Me. Don't stay stuck in your loss. Look a little higher and see that I have everything you need. Don't avoid Me. I am the only One who can truly help you and heal your heart."

It's been a vicious cycle since I lost Curt. I want to hide from my pain, and then God helps me to see that I need Him. So I steer back to the path I've driven on many times before. This path takes me to where I submit and trust my Lord. And there I find peace and hope, and the heaviness in my heart lifts. But just like the disciples couldn't stay on the Mount of Transfiguration no matter how wonderful it was (Matthew 17), I, too, must continuously re-engage with my life and responsibilities. Coming to Jesus once is never enough. Life happens and I get distracted and busy, so I must keep returning to that path with the ruts in the road from my frequent travel to that spot reserved for Jesus and me.

Curt told me the story of how his dad learned to drive a team of horses when he was a young boy. Curt's grandfather told his son to steer the horses so the wagon wheels will roll in the ruts in the dirt road that leads to home. Once the wheels were in the ruts, the horses would pretty much steer themselves. This is the subject of this poem that Curt wrote.

> He was young
> He was eager
> Given the reins
> Told it wouldn't be hard
> to drive the team
> down the wagon trail.
> Get the wheels in the ruts, son.
> It will pretty much steer itself.
> Pretty reassuring,
> Life in the ruts.
> — Curt Dalaba ©2018

By making it a habit to run to Jesus and telling Him that I trust Him, has created ruts in the road of my grief journey. Now that my grief is no longer constant but comes in unanticipated and violent waves, I find the ruts are helping me steer more quickly to the place I find relief. When I follow the ruts that my faith in God has created, I get much more than a Band-Aid from Him. He places His hand on me again, and I am whole even though half of me is gone. God fills the half that's missing. God makes me complete again. I sense that He's pleased that I have faith in Him. "Without faith, it is impossible to please God." (Hebrews 11:6 NIV)

> It's not like there is a faith meter or something. We will not be measured by how much faith we have like it's win or lose. No, God shows us what He expects, and what He expects cannot be accomplished in the energy of the flesh; it is a fruit of the Spirit. The only way this is accessed is through faith. Without faith you cannot see what is available, grab what is available, and use what is available. The eyes of faith broaden the horizons of my perspective. What we do to please God can only be accomplished through faith—and that's why without it you cannot.
> — Curt Dalaba, Journal Entry

I want to please God with how I process my grief. Sometimes I fail in this. I thank God for His mercy and grace. He forgives me and helps me return to the ruts in the road that lead me to where I find true comfort. It's only in trusting Him.

I think the reason I only find peace when I'm trusting God is that by doing so, I'm letting go of my will and submitting to His plan for my life. Too often I want to tell God how He should do things, and then I want to see Him answer that prayer. But Jesus taught us to pray, "Your Kingdom come, Your will be done, on earth as it is in heaven." (Matthew 6:10 NIV)

Several months before Curt was diagnosed with cancer, I felt impressed to pray those words every morning during my prayer time. Was God preparing me to accept the bitter loss of my husband? Was He preparing me to submit to His plan for my life? My guess would be, yes, He was.

I wanted God to heal Curt. Everything within me longed for that. I prayed God would not allow cancer to take him from me. But after reading Acts 3:16 NIV this week, I wonder if the person God wants to heal is me. "By faith in the name of Jesus, this man whom you see and know was made strong. It is Jesus's name and the faith that comes through him that has given this complete healing to him, as you can all see."

I believe that my faith in Jesus will make me strong and heal my broken heart because He has given me a new perspective that this earth is a place of preparation for eternity. My greatest goals should never be for this life, but for the life that awaits me in heaven. Everything I do or say or think should be with eternity in view. So I want God's will for my life. He's preparing me for all that is yet to come.

Aim at heaven, and you will get earth thrown in.
Aim at earth, and you get neither.
— C.S. Lewis

Lord, help me surrender my will to You. Help me accept Your will for my life and allow you to heal my heart. Let Your Kingdom come, and Your will be done on Earth as it is in heaven.

CHAPTER SEVENTEEN

Letting Go and Moving Forward

The loss of my husband has caused me to take a step back and review my life. I've become more introspective. This week, I thought back to when I first received the call to the ministry. I was twelve years old when I had a strong impression—possibly the first time I realized the Lord was speaking to me—that I would be a pastor's wife.

Nothing changed in my life after that. I stored the information in my heart and figured that if God wanted me to be a pastor's wife, He would make it happen. Besides, what if I got it wrong?

I attended a German-speaking Assemblies of God church of about sixty-five people. We had a fun youth

Facing Tomorrow Without You

group, but all the boys were like brothers to me. Not only did I attend a small church, I also lived in a small town. My opportunities for meeting men who were entering the ministry were probably almost nonexistent.

Well, I can tell you that God will accomplish whatever He sets out to do. Several years later, as Curt and his family drove home to Ohio after the Assemblies of God General Council meetings in San Antonio, strangers in the car passing them on the highway waved enthusiastically.

Curt's family waved back, of course, but wondered why this family was so friendly.

When the Dalaba family arrived at the next rest stop, Curt recognized the people from the car that had passed them. (I think Curt had a photographic memory. When he saw a face, he never forgot it.) He went up to greet them.

As they talked, the husband mentioned that he was the pastor of a German Assemblies of God church in Ohio.

Curt told them he had recently returned from a short-term mission's trip in Germany.

This pastor and his wife were thrilled to hear that Curt spoke fluent German. They told him about a German church in New Jersey that needed a pastor.

Curt wasn't interested, but they insisted he allow the Assemblies of God German District Superintendent to contact him. He finally agreed. Long story short, Curt became *my* pastor in New Jersey after "coincidentally" meeting this pastor from the German Assemblies of God District at a rest stop somewhere between Ohio and Texas.

Since Curt was a single pastor, he made it clear that he would never date a girl in his church.

Well, *I* would never pursue a man, so he had nothing to worry about where I was concerned. I wanted to find a man who wanted me in his life so

90

much that he would leap over any obstacle in his path.

Since Curt didn't have family who lived nearby, my mother gave him a standing invitation to join us for lunch in our home any Sunday he wasn't invited elsewhere. There was no need for him to eat alone on Sunday. He could always come over and sit at our table for a home-cooked meal.

Curt ended up joining us most Sundays. During those times around the table, a great friendship developed between us, but also an attraction we both fought against.

About fifteen months after he first arrived at our church, I received a call from him at work one day. He asked if I wanted to go out for lunch. That was our first date and the beginning of what became a wonderful marriage of thirty-three years.

Only God could take a girl from a small German church in a little town in New Jersey and cause her path to cross with a young pastor in Ohio, who had been in Germany for almost a year and was fluent in the German language. In no way should our paths ever have crossed in the natural, but God orchestrated a way.

Was it a coincidence that a young man without an ounce of German blood running through his veins gained a passion for the German language and taught himself without a teacher? He learned it so well that he could preach and teach in the German language. It was this ability that opened the door for us to meet.

The words Curt wrote in one of his Facebook posts were precious to me then, and even more so now: "God took me all the way back to New Jersey, just to find you. He knew I needed you, knew you would be the best friend I'd ever have, knew I needed everything about you, because we'd complement each other so well."

Our marriage was part of God's plan for my life. "Your eyes saw my unformed body; all the days ordained for me were written in your book before one of them came to be." (Psalm 139:16 NIV)

God had divinely arranged our meeting, but what about now? I'm no longer a pastor's wife, so what is my purpose? That calling has come to an end. What now? Did cancer destroy God's plan for my life?

The answer was a loud and resounding NO! Cancer cannot destroy God's plans because God is bigger than cancer. Psalm 139:16 tells us that even before we were born, all our days were ordained and written in a book —God's book. That includes the days Curt battled cancer and the days I struggled beside him to make him as comfortable as possible. Although we were shocked to discover he had cancer, God was not surprised. It was part of His sovereign plan for Curt. If that were not the case, it would turn God into a weak God, which we know He is *not*. He is all-powerful and all-knowing.

"Are not two sparrows sold for a penny? Yet not one of them will fall to the ground outside your Father's care. And even the very hairs of your head are all numbered. So don't be afraid; you are worth more than many sparrows." (Matthew 10:29–31 NIV)

If God cares for sparrows, how much more does he care for His children? If He knew the number of hairs on Curt's head, He certainly knew about cancer cells growing in his body. Nothing was hidden from God. But I also know that God loved Curt with an everlasting love that knew no bounds. Curt trusted in God's love and provision.

"How priceless is your unfailing love, O God! People take refuge in the shadow of your wings." (Psalm 36:7 NIV)

I believe when Curt was born, God already set his lifetime at sixty-five years, two months, and two days. God could have taken him to heaven as a baby. His health stats at birth pointed in that direction. He was born with an inherited heart disease and atelectasis of the lung. The doctor informed Curt's grandmother that he would not live. She called Curt's dad in Orange, MA, where he pastored a church, to let him know his son would soon die. Since Curt's mother had pre-eclampsia, she had stayed in Taunton, MA, with Curt's grandmother. Curt's Dad left almost immediately to drive the 100 miles to Taunton, but first he stopped at the home of friends who prayed with him.

No one had told Curt's mom yet about her baby's condition. The doctors decided to examine him one more time to be certain there was nothing they could do to help him before they informed his mother. When they checked his lungs and heart, everything sounded normal. Curt's Dad arrived and found his baby boy completely healthy. God had performed a miracle. It wasn't Curt's time to go.

In 2007, our daughter's senior year of high school, Curt was stung by a wasp while at home and went into anaphylactic shock. I didn't know what was happening except that he'd been stung by a wasp. He felt lightheaded and faint. I ran and grabbed two Benadryl capsules suspecting he had an allergic reaction and got him to swallow them. We didn't have an Epi-pen in the house because we didn't know he had any allergies. When I checked his blood pressure, it had dropped to 55/35 and he was almost unconscious at this point.

I called 911 and explained the situation. They kept me on the phone but told me that help was on the way. Later, my daughter informed me that I had been praying in tongues the entire time I was on the phone. I don't have a clear recollection of that. All I knew was that my husband was dying, and I needed God to help him. About ten minutes later, the EMTs arrived. They checked his blood pressure and it had risen to about 100/60, but they weren't taking any chances. They rushed him to the hospital.

The emergency room doctor asked me, "All you

gave him was Benadryl?" I nodded. "Yes, two of them."
I found out later that Benadryl could not have helped
him to survive such a severe anaphylactic shock as he
had experienced. In such cases, death can occur within
thirty minutes of onset. Curt's time hadn't come yet. A
few hours later, when the doctors were certain he was
okay, Curt walked out of the hospital. He lived to
perform his children's weddings, and he got to know his
three young grandchildren. He preached many more
sermons, mentored many pastors, and led people to the
Lord. His work wasn't done yet.

In 2018, two years before his death, we were on a
business trip in Houston, Texas, when Curt started
having terrible pain and began to vomit blood. I took
him by Uber to the emergency room. After an
examination, it turned out he needed to have his
gallbladder removed. We could do it there in Houston
or fly home and have it taken care of in Michigan. We
discussed it and decided to have the surgery in
Houston.

The surgery took much longer than anticipated.
Later, the surgeon told us that they were unable to do
the laparoscopic procedure because the stone in Curt's
gallbladder was the size of an orange. It required a large
incision to get the gallbladder out. The surgeon said he
had never seen a gallstone that huge in his many years
of performing this surgery. He actually took a picture of
it and couldn't wait to show his colleagues. Then he
told us that if we had chosen to fly home, Curt would
most certainly have died. Again, it wasn't his time to go.

But in 2020, the story ended quite differently. The
news went from bad to worse. This time, Curt *had*
reached the number of days allotted to him and it was
his time to go home.

When we married, God knew that after thirty-three
years and thirteen days, my heart would shatter into a
million pieces. He knew I'd be a widow before we had a

chance to retire together.

It seems cruel that God would allow this to happen to His children, but who are we to question Him? Remember, He didn't spare His Son, either. God knew the reason His Son had to suffer and die. He also knew death wasn't the end. There would be a resurrection. God knows things we cannot fathom. He has a sovereign plan that is truly best for us for all eternity.

It reminds me of Joseph and his brothers. The brothers wanted to get rid of him. They did a despicable thing when they sold him as a slave and then allowed their father to believe his son had died. But even then, God was still in control. He could have stopped them, but He didn't. God had a plan, and He used sinful men to accomplish it.

> I am Joseph, your brother, whom you sold into slavery in Egypt. But don't be upset, and don't be angry with yourselves for selling me to this place. It was God who sent me here ahead of you to preserve your lives. This famine that has ravaged the land for two years will last five more years, and there will be neither plowing nor harvesting. God has sent me ahead of you to keep you and your families alive and to preserve many survivors. So it was God who sent me here, and not you! And he is the one who made me an adviser to Pharaoh—the manager of this entire palace and governor of Egypt. (Genesis 45:4-8 NLT)

Joseph told his brothers that it wasn't their sin that had accomplished all this. It was God. In the same way, it wasn't cancer that took Curt. It was God. And it was God's will that I am a widow now and that I continue working for Him in partnership with the Holy Spirit, no longer as a pastor's wife, but always as a daughter of God.

Accepting this doesn't make the pain of grief disappear. Even today, as I read one of Curt's journal entries, I curled up on my bed and wept. It hurts. I miss him. But God is still in control. I am not living in God's Plan B for my life. I am still in God's Plan A. Accepting His sovereign plan helps me to relinquish my death grip on what used to be and accept God's continued plan for me. In His plan, I will find a priceless treasure.

In one of Curt's journal entries in 1999, he took a closer look at Matthew 13:44 NIV, "The kingdom of heaven is like a treasure hidden in a field. When a man found it, he hid it again, and then in his joy went and sold all he had and bought that field."

> It's very hard to give up what you have until you've found something better. We think of this very often in terms of money but think of some of the things we cherish; habits, patterns of thought, methods of operation. We don't give them up until we find something better.

> But you say, "I've found Jesus, so why do I still battle?" It has to do with the value—placed worth —that He holds in our lives.

> Seek first the Kingdom of God and His righteousness—love God first. The Kingpin—the central point.

> "Sell all we have" means giving up—not only the painful consequences of dearly held habits, patterns of thought, methods of behavior, but also the root possession. "I wish I could do this or that and not feel guilty. I wish I could do this and not mess things up or complicate things."

> He must increase; I must decrease. The small "g"

god must come off its pedestal.

The Kingdom of heaven is a priceless treasure that is to be desired above all else. The man had to pay a price for it. It is free; it just costs us everything we have.
— Curt Dalaba, Journal Entry, 1999

Accepting God's sovereign plan is relinquishing my will for His. If you've recently lost a loved one, it may take time before you can relinquish. God understands. He will work with you. But eventually, you will have to let go of the past so you can move forward.

I'm not saying I will forget Curt. That's not even possible, nor do I want to let go of my memories of him. His life and ministry influenced my life and made me who I am today. I thank God almost daily that I was blessed to be Curt Dalaba's wife. No woman was more blessed than I was. But just like Tarzan had to let go of one vine as he grabbed the next one so he could keep moving forward, I must let go of the past to keep moving forward.

Here is the wonderful and exciting part. Curt isn't in the past. He's moved forward into eternity. By letting go of the past, I'm moving forward into God's plan— *with* Curt. We are in different worlds now but still submitted to God and His sovereign will. And one day, we will meet again. Not in the past, but in the future.

The past is now a beautiful memory. It's okay to remember and treasure the memories. They give us reasons to worship and praise God for how He has blessed us and all He's brought us through. But we are not done yet. That's why we're still here. There are more people whose lives we must touch, and God wants to use us.

"... But one thing I do: Forgetting what is behind and straining toward what is ahead, I press on toward the goal to win the prize for which God has called me heavenward in Christ Jesus." (Philippians 3:13-14 NIV)

CHAPTER EIGHTEEN

Lessons Learned in the Dark

When driving home from the grocery store a few months ago, I went through a four-way stop sign. That's never happened to me before. It wasn't until I heard the blast of a horn that I realized what I'd done. Thank God, it wasn't a close call or anything like that, but it could have been.

After that incident, I looked up *widow brain*, something a friend had first mentioned. I had no idea there was a term for what I was feeling. The symptoms are forgetfulness, extreme sadness, brain fog, irritability, fatigue or exhaustion, numbness, and nausea. I've had each of those symptoms at some point since Curt passed

Facing Tomorrow Without You

away. It explained the foggy and disconnected feeling I struggled with.

Last Friday, I went grocery shopping and used the self-checkout lane. I had added some items to the cart that I didn't urgently need. I just didn't want to run out. The two items were crunchy peanut butter and marshmallow fluff, so I could make a fluffernutter sandwich if the mood hit me.

Since Curt's family is from Massachusetts, he introduced me to the fluffernutter sandwich that is popular in New England and originated in the state where Curt was born.

Anyway, almost two days later, I realized that I didn't have the crunchy peanut butter or the marshmallow fluff anywhere in the kitchen. I checked the trunk of my car just in case I had forgotten to unload a bag. Empty. It was then I realized two additional items were missing. I must have left one bag of groceries at the store checkout. Since it was Sunday morning, I decided to go to church and not let it bother me.

On Monday, I called the store. They suggested I come in, and they would look up my purchase receipt in their computer.

At the customer service desk, they tapped into their computer some numbers from the digital receipt, and indeed, they had restocked all the items I'd bought.

I had never left paid groceries at a store checkout counter before. Widow brain? I imagined that was exactly what I was dealing with.

Grief is the strangest thing ever. Nothing seems quite the same. Reading books about the grieving process has taught me that after you lose a loved one, you may find yourself fearful that you will lose someone else you love. Since the worst imaginable thing has happened, what's to keep it from happening again to another of your loved ones?

Although I still occasionally dealt with this fear, I also gained new insight. What I feared most, had happened. My husband was gone. My future was upside down. But I hadn't fallen apart. I had now lived ten months without Curt, and I was still breathing, eating, living, loving, and yes, even laughing sometimes. I didn't know how it was possible, but I had survived. And I felt more courageous and stronger.

My trust in God had deepened. Choosing to trust God at the beginning of this journey had made all the difference. Even with a broken heart and tears running down my face, even as I shouted that I couldn't understand. Just a simple step of faith—saying, "I trust You, God. Even now, I choose to trust You." That step planted my wavering faith in rich soil where it had all it needed to grow as God shone the light of His Word on that dark, cold ground, warming it with His devoted love. The Apostle Paul was right; I do not grieve as one who has no hope (1 Thessalonians 4:13).

My determination to focus on Heaven—learn more about it—and study the book of Revelation were two key factors that helped my faith to grow. Since I lost Curt, I have fixed my eyes on eternity like never before. I found myself reading the Bible and especially the Psalms like a lover devours love letters from the person he adores.

When I finally reach the last day ordained for me on this earth, God will be faithful to take me home. My heart leaps with joy at the thought. I don't relish dying, but death doesn't scare me as it once had. The goal of eternity with God has made me more courageous. This sinful world will wreak havoc and cause many more tears to flow, but it is well with my soul, and my future is secure in my Heavenly Father's love. Psalm 90:12 says, "So teach us to number our days, that we may get a heart of wisdom." Every day on this earth matters. How will I fill those days?

> The sweetest songs of earth have been sung in sorrow. The richest things in character, have been reached through pain.
>
> — J.R. Miller [1]

No one wants to face the sorrow that creates depth of character and gives deeper insight. But when you find yourself in the darkest phase of your life, wasting the grief on bitterness would be the greatest loss. There is much to learn from pain. The most profound lesson is how deep faith can grow in times like these. Bitterness leads to regret. But as I relinquish my dreams to God, He takes me to new heights. I can never reach the pinnacle of faith without walking through the darkest valley fully surrendered to Him.

I'm not the same person Curt left behind last September. If he and I could take a walk together today, I'm sure he'd notice I've changed. I can only imagine the change in him now that he's seen Jesus and knows the answers to the questions we still have.

> "Don't doubt in the dark what you've learned in the light," they say. What they don't tell you is that life's vital lessons aren't learned in the light at all, but in the darkest pit. Like Jacob, I have been given a new identity: everything I know about God, I know from the perspective of a father who has lost a daughter. This, as it turns out, is a helpful perspective from which to view the Bible, because the God we worship is also a father who suffered the death of a child. I dare not forget in the light what I've learned in the dark.

Like countless others who have suffered loss, I've received a gift—the sudden, clear, accurate realization that something is vitally wrong with this world. Our lives, like so many things in this world, are transitory; without God's ultimate meaning, there is no meaning. Creation is groaning, says Paul, subjected to futility, eagerly longing for God to straighten things out. An adequate theology will not avoid this truth but embrace it.

— Luke Veldt [2]

We live in a fallen world. Each one of us will encounter grief at some point if we haven't already. It's unavoidable. The best way to prepare for grief is to draw close to God now, have such a tight relationship with Him, and know His Word. This will lay the foundation of faith which you will need when that time comes.

I've reached the ten-month mark of Curt's passing. Just writing that sentence brings such intense pain that my eyes well with tears. Curt didn't want to leave me any more than I wanted him to go. We didn't get a choice in the matter. I only get to choose how I'll respond.

Curt wrote the following in his journal twenty-eight years ago during the time we lived in Germany for four years. He sometimes had the opportunity to preach at a church in Heidelberg, which was about a two-and-a-half-hour drive from our home in the Nuremberg area. The people in this church were all from the Middle East.

My husband was diligent about prayer and Bible reading. He never neglected his time with the Lord, not even on vacation. His relationship with God took top priority each day, and no doubt it made him the wonderful husband, father, and excellent Bible teacher that he was. As you read this portion of his journal, you will see his unrelenting desire for more of God.

I want this new year to draw me much closer to the Lord. I want to walk closer to Him than ever before. More Word. More Prayer. May He fill my heart with greater goodness, purity, focus, determination, love, etc. As regards our future, we must leave it in God's hands, knowing that at the right time He will make it clear; just as he did in getting us here in the first place.

We left for Heidelberg at around 12:45. It snowed off and on the whole way. There was a good crowd in church. The real surprise came when they asked me to go upstairs to pray with two men that wanted to accept Jesus. They were serious. The groundwork was already laid. They repented and asked Jesus into their hearts. It was a great moment.

Isn't it like the Lord to give encouragement when we need it most? We don't know what our future holds, but I'm determined to take it one day at a time.
—— Curt Dalaba, Journal Entry, January 1, 1995

God brought us through so much, guiding us every step of the way, one day at a time. Now I'm walking out the remainder of my days alone—yet not alone. I still have my family, my friends, church fellowship, and I'm meeting new people as I continue to move forward. Most of all, I have God. He promised that He'd never leave me. So I'm doing my best to continue to live my life one day at a time. Worry and fear are my enemy. "So do not fear, for I am with you; do not be dismayed, for I am your God. I will strengthen you and help you; I will uphold you with my righteous right hand." (Isaiah 41:10 NIV)

I want to advance God's Kingdom every day of my life. As long as I'm on Earth, I still have the opportunity to help encourage and strengthen people's faith, lead unbelievers to God, and work wherever God places me, especially in my family. I still have time to store up treasures in heaven. Remember what Matthew 6:19–21 NIV says. "Do not store up for yourselves treasures on earth, where moths and vermin destroy, and where thieves break in and steal. But store up for yourselves treasures in heaven, where moths and vermin do not destroy, and where thieves do not break in and steal. For where your treasure is, there your heart will be also."

I have fixed my heart and my gaze on Jesus, my Savior and eternity with Him. One day, I'll understand why I had to grieve. But until that day comes, I choose to trust God about my past, my present, and my future. Although I must live in this broken world, God is always in control, and He loves me. I will cry when the pain overwhelms me, but I will always come back to this: I trust You, God.

[1]. J.R. Miller, The Ministry of Comfort, 2014

[2]. Luke Veldt, Maimed By God: Wrestling, Groaning, Blessing, Written in Tears, 2010, pg 143

CHAPTER NINETEEN

My Birthday, Another First

The morning of my first birthday without Curt, I lay awake in bed with my eyes shut. A memory entered my mind of something that happened on a Sunday afternoon over thirty-five years ago. My family had enjoyed lunch around our dining room table with our pastor as our guest, who happened to be Curt. Of course, we had no idea what the future would bring. He was our new pastor and now, our friend.

After lunch, while my mom puttered around in the kitchen and everyone had gone their separate ways, Curt and I sat at the dining room table playing a game of Scrabble. Most of the tiles were on the board. We each had a couple more tiles to play. An X lay just two spaces from a triple word square. It was Curt's turn.

I faced a dilemma. Curt was ahead of me by several points, and my two remaining tiles were an S and an E. Did I dare use the word "sex" to win the game? I mean, this was my pastor—a single, good-looking man. On the other hand, that one word would turn the game in my favor. Of course, maybe Curt would take that spot and remove the temptation. I sat with bated breath to see what he would do.

Unaware of the battle going on in my head, Curt took his turn. He placed his tiles far from the X.

It was my turn now. I looked at my tiles for a moment longer. If I threw caution to the wind, I'd gain thirty points and win the game. The competitive side of me overpowered any shyness. I placed S and E in front of the X and held my breath.

Curt's head shot up. He looked at me in exaggerated shock.

My cheeks grew warm, but I couldn't hold back a victor's grin.

He burst out laughing.

That may have been the moment I fell in love with him. His sense of humor was so fun.

As I lay in bed on the morning of my first birthday without Curt, it dawned on me that I was smiling. The memory, so precious and beautiful, filled me with gratitude and joy that lasted all day. What should have been a terrible day of sorrow, completely turned around with one memory. I hadn't thought of that incident for at least a decade or longer. Just a simple memory, but God used it to change an entire day.

No one can comfort us like God can. His healing oil reaches into the deepest crevices of our brokenness and pain.

"He heals the brokenhearted and bandages their wounds." (Psalm 147:3 NLT)

"Blessed are those who mourn, for they will be

comforted." (Matthew 5:4 NASB)

I thank God for special times like this one when He intervened. But there are still days when God doesn't spare me the sadness of my new circumstances.

Recently, I attended the funeral of a man from our former church. When Curt resigned, Bob pulled him aside and told him, "Wherever you go, I want you to come back and do my funeral." This precious saint passed away in August (eleven months after Curt's death), only a few years shy of turning 100, and instead of Curt doing his funeral, I imagine Curt greeted Bob at the heavenly gates.

As I sat at the funeral, these thoughts ran through my mind. I enjoyed seeing so many people from our former church—people whose lives had intertwined with ours for a season of eighteen years. Curt had officiated many funerals in that funeral home. Countless times, he and I arrived there together and left together, but this time I entered and exited alone. This is my cross to bear, and God does not spare me from all the pain just like he didn't spare so many who have walked this path before me. But He is teaching me valuable lessons.

A dear friend directed me to Tim Challies's blog about two months into my grief journey. He is a pastor in Canada who lost his son while he was away at college about one month after I lost Curt. His words are raw but so encouraging.

> I'm not the same man I was on November 2. I'm deeply wounded, deeply scarred, deeply broken. Yet I know it's God who decreed this suffering, and I accept it as something meaningful, something precious. I'm eager to learn and to apply its painful lessons. I'm eager to be made better by it. [1]

I think the key to growing in faith amid grief is to remember the character of God. If Eve had taken the time to contemplate God's friendship with Adam and her—His faithfulness, His love, His kindness—I imagine she would not have been tempted by the devil's lies.

During grief, it would be so easy to wallow in my pain and allow bitterness to grow. Why do my friends get to grow old with their husbands, but I can't? Why did my children have to lose their dad so soon? Why would God allow my grandchildren to never know what a wonderful grandfather they had? Why, why, why? If I stay focused on these unanswered questions, I will get stuck in a pit of self-pity.

I think Eve began to feel very sorry for herself when the devil pointed out that God was depriving her. It was a lie, of course, but she believed it. Her ingratitude caused greed to grow in her heart. If only she had remembered the truth about God. He had been generous to them. He withheld nothing except one tree in the garden. Her ingratitude caused her to become blind to her countless blessings and focus only on the one thing she couldn't have.

I'm certainly not saying that I'm better than Eve. Not at all. I know my own weaknesses only too well. But I can read about Eve's mistake and learn from it. That's something Eve didn't have—examples to follow.

The enemy of our souls loves nothing more than for us to turn our anger on God for taking our loved ones away from us. The devil wants us to focus on what we lost and blind us to the blessings that are still around us. This kind of response causes the devil to do a happy dance, knowing he can keep us imprisoned in our misery for as long as our anger lasts. He will feed that anger and keep us trapped forever if we allow it.

As Americans, we grow up hearing that we have the

right to life, liberty, and the pursuit of happiness. It's a right we cherish and protect. But applying that sort of pride to things that matter for eternity puts us in opposition to the teachings of Jesus. He told His disciples, "And whoever does not take his cross and follow me is not worthy of me. He who has found his life will lose it, and he who has lost his life for My sake will find it." (Matthew 10:38–39 NIV)

When God called Curt home, I stood at a T in the road. Two options lie before me. I had to choose either my innate or imagined rights, which would justify anger at God for causing me to lose my happiness, or I could choose to die to my plans, submit to God, and even embrace the cross, the burden, the heartache, and the loneliness with humility and trust.

The thing staring me in the face—what I could not ignore—was the character of God. No matter what had happened to me, God was still the same. He did not leave me or forsake me. (Deuteronomy 31:6) I know that, although I have to walk through the valley of the shadow of death, I have nothing to fear, for God is with me. (Psalm 23:4) I know that when He has tested me, I will come forth as gold. (Job 23:10) I know that God's goodness and unfailing love will pursue me all the days of my life, and I will dwell in the house of the Lord forever. (Psalm 23:6) And because I know my God, I am confident that after I have suffered a little while, He will restore, support, and strengthen me, and He will place me on a firm foundation. (1 Peter 5:10)

So on the morning of my birthday, as I climbed out of bed still smiling from that sweet memory of what I had the privilege to experience long ago, I began to get ready for my day. As I sat before the make-up mirror, my heart bubbled over with joy. I closed my eyes and raised my hands to the heavens to worship God by singing:

All that thrills my soul is Jesus,
He means more than life to me
And the fairest of ten thousand,
In my blessed Lord I see.

[1]. Tim Challies, "I'm not the same man I was on November 2," Grief Should Always Make Us Better, January 4, 2021, Challies.com

CHAPTER TWENTY

Entering the Second Year

I have now entered the second year of my grief journey. Before I share more, let me remind you that everyone's grief journey is not the same. I think a lot has to do with personality, the depth of the relationship you lost, and how vital that person was to your happiness in this life. So, my story might be different from your story.

As the first anniversary approached, I braced myself for it. More than the actual date of Curt's departure, I dreaded the day before that date—when they had moved Curt into palliative care. As the anniversary approached, I had flashbacks of all that transpired before Curt's final day on Earth and the pain we were forced to endure—the shock. It was a day of heartbreak from beginning to end.

Cancer is vicious, and it unexpectedly robs you of the time you thought you still had. Curt wanted to say more but lost the ability to do so. I wanted to say more, but shock kept the words bottled up and wouldn't release them. We wanted this valley of the shadow of death to end, but my children and I clung to each moment, not wanting Curt to depart. We couldn't have it both ways.

This year, as the day before the anniversary of Curt's death approached, all these images plagued me, especially as I lay in my bed at night. I could still picture the room, the nurse, the lack of beeping machines because there was no need to sustain life. The awful silence. It was time to let go.

Hoping to make the first anniversary more bearable for ourselves, my children, grandchildren, and I chose to vacation in Florida, far from Michigan and all the painful memories. Curt's parents and sister live in Florida, so we were able to visit with them, which was a precious time for all of us. We purposely shared happy memories and made wonderful new memories. It gave us much joy to recall the many tender and funny moments with Curt. We laughed, and sometimes we wiped away tears, but whatever the emotion of the moment, the longing for what we lost never left our hearts.

Now, I'm almost one month into my second year without Curt. Is it less painful than the first? So far, I can't say that it is. It's different. I don't cry as much as last year, especially those first six months of seemingly endless tears. But the fact that Curt isn't coming back is sinking in like never before. And the length of my life stretches out disappointingly long into my future. Please don't misunderstand. I don't have a death wish. I'm still here, so my work isn't done, and God has more for me to learn and do. It's just that I've lost that sparkly feeling about life. It all feels somehow anticlimactic.

The grief journey is complicated and complex. For most of us, the pain doesn't end after one year. I've talked to some widows who told me it took them seven and even eight years or longer to finally feel healed. I was privileged to visit recently with a widow who lost her husband over forty years ago. What a blessing she was to me. Her eyes filled with tears as she talked about her husband. I realized that you never stop missing someone you deeply loved. No matter where life takes you, your heart cannot forget the one who embodied most of your happiness.

Thank God I'm doing much better now than at the beginning. But the waves of grief still come unexpectedly. Seemingly out of nowhere, the longing becomes intense—to feel Curt's hand in mine, look into his eyes, hear his words of encouragement, take a long walk together, sit quietly in the same room or have a deep conversation, laugh about something adorable our grandchildren did. The list goes on and on. Of course, such a loss will not disappear in one year. I might not receive complete healing until heaven, but I'm okay with that. I have God, and with Him as my partner, I can make it through anything. Grief doesn't diminish, but God helps us to grow around our grief.

Paul's words, so often quoted, ring truer to me than ever before. "For I can do everything through Christ, who gives me strength." (Philippians 4:13 NLT)

When I felt weak during the first year of my grief journey, I asked God for strength. When I felt lonely, I asked Him to fill the loneliness, not with another person, but with Himself. I asked Jesus to be my partner. It wasn't something I did only once, but over and over again. "Keep on asking, and you will receive what you ask for. Keep on seeking, and you will find. Keep on knocking, and the door will be opened to you." (Matthew 7:7 NLT)

If I allow Jesus to be my partner, I will desire what He desires. And what Jesus longs for is that everyone will spend eternity with Him. He wants me to do my part to rescue the perishing. But my world has become so much smaller without Curt. In my opinion, Curt would have done a far better job of telling people about Jesus. His sphere of influence was greater. His abilities and Scriptural knowledge exceeded mine exponentially. But who am I to question God's wisdom? So, I continue with my tasks.

At the end of August and early September, I helped my daughter and her family move from Connecticut to Massachusetts. As I filled boxes with their belongings and treasures, my mind swept back to when Curt and I packed all we owned to move from New Jersey to Michigan, then a few years later from Michigan to Germany, and then several more moves after that. Curt was an organized person. He taught me much about packing. I thought of how fun it would be if he were here to help us with this move. He would have had us laughing because he could find humor in almost any situation. I miss that about him.

While packing in Connecticut, I had earphones in my ears so I wouldn't disturb my daughter, who was working virtually in the other room for her job. I listened to YouTube as several Christians shared their near-death experiences. There was one common thread that stood out to me in each of their stories. In their life review, the only thing that seemed to matter to Jesus were the things they had done to help others. The unnoticed acts of kindness, the words that brightened someone's day. It all came down to love, joy, peace, forbearance, kindness, goodness, faithfulness, gentleness, and self-control (Galatians 5:22-23 NIV). By serving others, we please God. Didn't Jesus illustrate this for us when He washed the disciples' feet?

"After washing their feet, he put on his robe again

and sat and asked, "Do you understand what I was doing? You call me 'Teacher' and 'Lord,' and you are right, because that's what I am. And since I, your Lord and Teacher, have washed your feet, you ought to wash each other's feet. I have given you an example to follow. Do as I have done to you." (John 13:12-15 NLT)

It's much less complicated than people sometimes try to make it. If I want to please my Lord, I must serve the ones Jesus has placed in my life. It's that simple and that difficult because serving requires dying to myself. I have found that often when the opportunity arises to serve, the timing is lousy. I must stop what I'm doing for the benefit of someone else. I'm required to have a servant's heart.

Last week, I took my dog for a walk. He's a mostly black, fun-loving, fifteen-pound, nine-year-old Yorkipoo named Scooter. As we walked through our neighborhood, a long-haired dachshund rushed toward us, leash dangling from his collar, and his owner giving chase. I knew that dog. He's the one who bit my dog in the past. His owner didn't stand a chance of reaching him before he got to us.

Wanting to protect my dog, I lifted him into my arms and started running toward his owner, hoping the dachshund would follow and the lady could grab his leash. I wasn't afraid he'd bite me. He had an issue with Scooter, not me.

Unfortunately, my "big idea" (as my grandson would say) wasn't so great. The dachshund ran in front of me and then around me, wrapping his leash around my legs. I felt myself falling in the middle of the neighborhood road, and there was nothing I could do to stop. As fast as I landed, I stood back up again, but I lost my grip on Scooter.

The two dogs were growling at each other. At this point, I didn't bother pulling Scooter away but let him fight his own battle, which he did valiantly with his snarls. It seemed neither dog dared attack. It was like they were sizing each other up to see whose growl was biggest.

At that point, the owner finally arrived and grabbed her dog's leash. She apologized profusely.

I assured her I only had some minor scrapes, nothing worth mentioning.

She continued apologizing.

I gently placed my hand on her arm and told her again, "Please, don't worry about it. I'm fine." I felt sorry for her because I imagined how awful and embarrassed I'd feel if that had happened to me.

We parted ways, and I continued my walk.

Although the scrapes on my elbow, hand, and knee burned, I felt unexplainable joy. Why, I didn't know. I reviewed what had just happened, trying to make sense of my elated emotions. Soon the answer came. God was pleased with how I had responded to this lady in my neighborhood. I don't know anything about her life. I only know which house she lives in, that she's married, and has, at least, two teenage or young adult sons. Yet God knows every detail of her life, and He loves her.

I felt God speak to my heart that this is how He wants to use me in His Kingdom. He wants me to love the people with whom I rub shoulders and come into contact. That is the work I must do.

I guess I had to get scraped up to be in a position for God to remind me of my calling. Kindness, compassion, patience, all the fruits of the Spirit. It's every believer's calling. Only heaven will reveal how our lives impacted those around us.

CHAPTER TWENTY-ONE

The Christmas Assurance

All the lights, music, laughter, and good cheer of the season felt like a distant memory never to be recaptured on that first Christmas without my husband. Would this holiday ever delight me again as it had before my loss? Was Christmas ruined forever?

I had just come through a year of dealing with my loss, and I found myself approaching another Christmas. But I viewed this Christmas from a new perspective. I decorated my artificial evergreen with glass balls and ribbons. Multiple mini lights twinkled and shone brightly outside my house for all my neighbors to see, but the ache for what I lost continued to gnaw.

Late one evening, I walked past my living room, where the Christmas tree stood by the front window. It was dark outside, and I'd forgotten to turn the switch on to light up the tree. How strange. You see, I had always made certain those lights were on to greet Curt when he drove up after a day at the office. I wanted him to feel the warmth of home even before he entered. When he walked through the door of our house, with the smells of Christmas wafting in the air and carols softly playing in the background, I would greet him with a kiss and tell him how happy I was to have him home. But without that incentive, I stood in the dark front room, flipped on the lights of the tree late that evening, and looked out at the empty driveway where his car would never park again.

I turned my gaze to the dark sky and asked the question for the hundredth time, "Why?"

I wasn't looking for an answer. It was more of a declaration of grief. I'd been doing so well, experiencing days on end without tears. I had continued to move forward. But with Christmas upon us, memories and melancholic emotions were rising to the surface again. It's normal, I know, but I don't want to stay in this place of sadness.

1 Thessalonians 4:13 NIV says, "Brothers and sisters, we do not want you to be uninformed about those who sleep in death, so that you do not grieve like the rest of mankind, who have no hope."

What is the hope we have? We have the hope of a reunion with our loved ones because Jesus, God's only begotten Son, came to Earth, died on a cross, and rose again. There would never have been a reunion for Curt and me without God's sacrifice of His Son for our sake. Before Jesus's death and resurrection, we were doomed for eternal separation from God—eternity in hell—and separation from each other. That was our destiny. If not for Jesus, September 25, 2020, would have been our final farewell. I would have to live here knowing I would never see Curt again. There would have been no songs of worship to God around Curt's death bed, only tears, agony, and despair.

But on that glorious and holy night, when our Savior was born, hope entered this world. The powers of darkness—Satan and his demons—trembled at His arrival. They had to find a way to kill this baby. He couldn't have the opportunity to grow. They schemed and planned. They killed and destroyed, but they could not stop God's plan. A helpless child with parents of no great significance could not be harmed by the rulers of Earth or the powers of darkness when God protected them. His plan was to save souls and offer mankind an unimaginably amazing future for all eternity, and He would not be defeated. What Satan stole in the garden, God returned to us in a manger and on a cross.

As I stood before the Nativity scene in my living room, I looked at the Christ child with new eyes, and my heart filled with unspeakable joy. Because of that holy night, I will see Curt again. We didn't say goodbye forever. Because God came to Earth and dwelt among men, died, and rose again, there will be a reunion for all of us with our loved ones. I will one day fall on my knees before my Savior, with Curt kneeling beside me, and we will raise our voices in worship to Jehovah God Almighty and the Savior of the world.

No, Christmas will never be the same again. How can it? So much has changed. But I celebrate Christmas with a deeper appreciation because of my loss. I value the worth of God's gift to me with greater and deeper understanding. Like the shepherds and wisemen who came and worshiped their Savior, I bend my knees and lift my hands to worship my Lord this Christmas season.

Thank you, Jesus, for my salvation. Thank you, God, for a promised reunion. Thank you that life doesn't end here. Thank you that I will one day spend all eternity with You.

After all these years of attending church during the Christmas season, I have heard and read the verses in Isaiah 9 countless times. Many Christmas greeting cards contain these words. But it's not enough that I hear or read what the prophet said. Only when I take the time to meditate on this powerful prophecy will my faith grow.

"For a child is born to us, a son is given to us. The government will rest on his shoulders. And he will be called: Wonderful Counselor, Mighty God, Everlasting Father, Prince of Peace. His government and its peace will never end. He will rule with fairness and justice from the throne of his ancestor David for all eternity. The passionate commitment of the LORD of Heaven's Armies will make this happen!" (Isaiah 9:6-7 NLT)

When I joined Curt in marriage, he made a commitment to me. He meant what he said, and I trusted his promise to me. He remained faithful to his vows to his last breath. Imagine how much more we can depend upon the "passionate commitment of the LORD of Heaven's Armies." He promised us eternity with Him, and He will do what He promised.

"Don't let your hearts be troubled. Trust in God, and trust also in me. There is more than enough room in my Father's home. If this were not so, would I have told you that I am going to prepare a place for you? When everything is ready, I will come and get you, so that you will always be with me where I am. And you know the way to where I am going." (John 14:1-4 NLT)

It's amazing and wonderful that we have this reassurance of a reunion with loved ones and an eternity with Jesus. But we are still living on this earth and have to get through this life, so waves of grief will come. As the holiday season progressed, I still had to continue to deal with my loss.

Following is a message I sent to my children on our second Christmas Eve without Curt. We all missed him so much. I longed to put my love for Curt into words, and I knew my children would be willing to read it. They knew how much Curt and I loved each other, so they understood my loss.

I carried all the gifts from my bedroom into the living room to put by the tree—something Dad and I used to do together. My phone dinged. It was a text from Uncle Robert with a beautiful song. I wept as I listened. I haven't grieved like this since probably September when you all went home after our wonderful vacation in Florida for our one-year anniversary of losing Dad.

I really didn't expect this Christmas to hit me this hard. I thought I cried enough tears last Christmas, but I think my heart forgot. Yet the grief is a bit different this year.

Last year, I clung to the hope that Jesus would return soon—maybe in less than a year—and I could be with Dad again. This year, I realize it could be many more years before our reunion.

Last year, it hurt to even think about Dad. Even good memories hurt. This year, I can almost see him walk into a room filled with family as he did so many times before. His eyes would seek mine out. We could communicate our love and connectedness with just one look into each other's eyes. My heart would reach out to his across the room. That brief moment was ours alone. And then we'd turn our attention to include everyone else into our world. Oh, how I long for Dad, my soulmate, tonight.

When it comes to grieving and healing, most of it is done in the deepest recesses of our hearts that are filled with all the memories and emotions of the past. It's a secret place. We don't even have words to describe the depth of emotion in that place. We just feel the void, the longing, and the immense love we can no longer express. It's a place of fulfillment because we had been given the most amazing gift—true, deep, abiding love. And it's the place of devastating longing for all we lost. No one can meet us there except God. Words are inadequate to fully describe that place. We must go there alone—but with God—and come to terms with our loss and accept what cannot be changed. And then we must ask God for the strength, will, and determination to keep moving forward.

Christmas is such a nostalgic time. We can't help looking backwards. But after Christmas comes a New Year—a new beginning. God will help me forward, but tonight I will weep for what was taken from me.

It's okay to grieve. God understands how much we hurt. But even while grieving, may the true meaning of Christmas fill our hearts with hope and joy. There will be a glorious reunion, and our hearts will be completely healed on that day.

CHAPTER TWENTY-TWO

What About the Promises?

For someone who had always trusted Scripture to be accurate and true, it rocked my world when I read my Bible seeking for comfort for my loss and came across verses that didn't make sense considering what our family had experienced. Some verses caused me to feel as though I'd been lied to or excluded. For example, "Lord my God, I called to you for help, and you healed me." (Psalm 30:2 NIV) Here's another one: "You may ask me for anything in my name, and I will do it." (John 14:14 NIV) We had called out to God. We had asked. Curt had been anointed with oil by the elders of our church, and they prayed for healing for him. We held prayer services and claimed the truth of Scripture in faith, believing for Curt's healing. But he died anyway.

We had prayed the same prayers over Curt that we prayed over others who came to us for healing prayers in the past. Many were healed, but Curt wasn't. Over a thousand people joined us in prayer for Curt, and still, he died. We didn't even get a short reprieve, like a remission from cancer that would have added a few more years to his life. Instead, his health steadily worsened until he was gone.

So when I read verses like Psalm 34:6 NLT, "In my desperation I prayed, and the Lord listened; he saved me from all my troubles," it seemed like, perhaps, the psalm didn't apply to everyone.

But I remembered Curt's words from long ago. "If Scripture doesn't make sense or seems to contradict itself, the problem isn't with Scripture; the problem is with my understanding of Scripture."

I asked the Lord what He meant when he said, "The thief comes only to steal and kill and destroy; I came so that they would have life and have it abundantly." (John 10:10 NASB) Although I had experienced abundant life for a large portion of my life, it was no longer true. My abundant life ended when I lost my husband, my closest and dearest friend, the other half of me. I felt robbed of the gift God had given to me.

I prayed, "God, please tell me what this means because I know Your Word is true, but it does *not* appear to be true in my life."

I'm sure God heard that question from many others before me and probably more times than anyone can count. He wasn't angry that I asked about something that was burning in my heart. Quite the opposite. I felt understood by Him, and I knew He would show me the answer when the time was right. In the meantime, I continued to read my Bible, pray, and worship Him. His answer would come eventually.

As the days went by, I thought about the disciples and how they enjoyed being with Jesus and trusted Him to deliver them from oppression. The truth began to slowly, piece by piece, settle into my mind.

The disciples and all of Jesus's other followers had been waiting so long for the Redeemer to appear. They, as well as their parents, grandparents, and great-grandparents had all heard the prophecies that foretold the Messiah's arrival. How joyful they must have been when they realized Jesus was, indeed, the Messiah, the Son of God, their Redeemer! He had arrived just as He promised. They would soon be free from the oppressive Roman government.

They must have felt perplexed and angry when the Roman soldiers came and grabbed Jesus to arrest Him and lead Him away. No wonder Peter slashed off the soldier's ear. He probably thought he would start the fight, and then Jesus would take over and call His legions of angels to overthrow that oppressive ruling power. Was this the moment they had been waiting for?

Instead, Jesus picked up the ear, placed it back on the side of the soldier's head, and healed him. Then He surrendered himself to the soldiers and allowed them to take Him away.

Peter wasn't ready to give up yet. I'm pretty certain he was an optimist. Jesus was still alive, so there was no reason to lose hope. Surely, He would save Himself and all of Israel too. Jesus must have a plan. There was still time. So Peter followed to see what would happen next.

Imagine the despair and confusion Peter and the other disciples must have felt as Jesus hung on the cross, stayed silent through all the mockery, and then took His final breath. They must have thought, *How is this possible? He was supposed to redeem us.* Instead, it seemed the Romans had won. Where was Israel's hope now? Until Jesus came, they had anticipated His arrival and their deliverance. But now, all was lost. It must have been the darkest, most hopeless, and loneliest moment in their lives.

However, we know the rest of the story. Three days later, Jesus arose! He didn't stay in the tomb, praise God! The disciples and other followers of Jesus finally understood that God's plan had never been about here and now. It had always been about eternity.

Before, the disciples had been too earthly minded to grasp the bigger picture. They'd waited for the Redeemer to come to save them from Rome, to give them abundant life on Earth.

God's plan was so much greater. He came to save us *all* from the oppression of Satan and this sinful world. He came to give us *all* everlasting life with Him in a place more spectacular than anything we've ever seen before. It was God's plan for us from the beginning. He came to give us so much more than we could ever imagine.

Now, when I read verses like Psalm 103:2-3 NIV, "Praise the Lord, my soul, and forget not all his benefits —who forgives all your sins and heals all your diseases," I know God's promises were never limited to this life alone. In fact, they were mostly intended for all eternity.

God's plan for Curt was so much greater. Curt has arrived where I long to be—in eternity with Jesus. And he is completely healed! "… No eye has seen, no ear has heard, and no mind has imagined what God has prepared for those who love him." (1 Corinthians 2:9 NLT)

An unimaginable inheritance awaits us. Oh, let that thought sink in. God, who is holy and all-powerful, our Savior and Redeemer, is *excited* to welcome us into eternity with Him! I long for that day with a longing that causes my heart to ache. *That* is when all of God's promises in Scripture for my life and for yours will at last be fulfilled.

CHAPTER TWENTY-THREE

My Favorite Scrooge

If there was one thing Curt was not, it was a scrooge. But he was the best Scrooge I ever saw on a stage. He was downright fantastic.

Today, as I drove alone in my car, twenty-six days until my third Christmas without Curt, a distant memory entered my mind, and I could almost clearly visualize some of the scenes from over thirty-three years ago. I was pregnant with our first child, and Curt was an associate pastor in a large church in Michigan. The music department was preparing a Christmas production, The Gospel According to Scrooge, and they asked Curt to play the part of Ebenezer Scrooge.

Whatever Curt did, he did well. He never shied

away from hard work, and it was no different with this play. Night after night, we went over the lines at home. I read the parts for all the other characters so he could insert his lines in the appropriate places. It wasn't enough for Curt to know his lines well. He also pushed himself to recite it with a beautiful British accent. Listening to him speak his lines was pure joy to any discerning ear.

The night of the production, I sat toward the front of the church and was mesmerized. Everyone did such a fine job, but Curt was outstanding. My heart swelled with pride.

I gently eased on the brake of my car as I approached an intersection, and my mind returned to the present, but a smile stayed on my face at the sweet recollection. I'm having more such moments now, when unexpected and long forgotten memories reappear. I allow them to linger in my thoughts and savor those echoes from the past.

We Did Not Know

we did not know
what we had
when we had you
with us long ago

and had we known
what we know now
we would have asked
one more question

staring at you
one more time
soaking in your visage
another snapshot in time

all you said
taken more seriously
all you did
viewed more lovingly

we did not know then
how short our time
together would be, always
believing for tomorrow

one day tomorrow stopped
I clamored for every thought
I ever had of you
and wrote them anew

upon my mind, so I
would not forget
and never ever let
escape my heart, yet I

wished I'd kept more
in secret store
of all you did and all you said
because I miss you still.
— Curt Dalaba ©2018

My children and I knew what we had. We valued Curt's guidance and advice. But even so, this poem rings true.

In this third year since Curt had to leave, there are moments when our past life together feels like a dream. Like it never really happened. Of course, when I see my children and grandchildren, the evidence of our marriage is only too obvious. But when I experience a specific remembrance that I hadn't thought about in decades, it feels like a gift. The memories help to make it all real again.

After the loss of a loved one, there is the fear of forgetting—of losing the memories. Often, we wish we had written more into our journals or taken more pictures or videos.

It's wonderful that our brains are amazing storage systems. Memories that seem out of reach can suddenly reappear as though they happened yesterday. It's okay to cherish those memories and see them as the gifts that they are.

In the book of Joshua in the Old Testament, we see that Moses was no longer on Earth, but he wasn't forgotten. Joshua was now the leader of the nation of Israel. Notice how God remembers His promise to Moses in Joshua 1:3 NIV, "I will give you every place where you set your foot, as I promised Moses."

This must have helped Joshua remember the things God had spoken to Moses. The things Joshua had learned from his mentor. It was probably a fond memory that now gave him courage.

I believe our memories can also encourage us. The memory of Curt playing Scrooge that I shared with you was certainly precious to me, but I only gave you the highlight of that memory. The little personal details that the memory awakened are priceless to me. Those tiny details are impactful and reassuring and all mine.

You see, God sees deep into our hearts and thoughts. He knows the questions we haven't voiced. It could be that we don't have the words to express our deepest concerns or unfinished business. Since Curt passed, there have been many one-sided conversations in my mind. I long for a chance to talk with him, even if only one more time, just to hear what he has to say. I long for his insights. All our marriage, I shared my thoughts and experiences with him, and he shared his with me. We discussed the details together. But we were robbed of the opportunity to discuss his death. What was it like when his spirit left his body? Does he know what we have faced since he's been gone? Can he see how our grandchildren are growing? Does he know they still mention him? Although having a conversation with Curt is impossible, that doesn't stop the questions from formulating in my mind. But God sees. He knows my thoughts.

"You have searched me, Lord, and you know me. You know when I sit and when I rise; you perceive my thoughts from afar. You discern my going and my lying down; you are familiar with all my ways. Before a word is on my tongue you, Lord, know it completely." (Psalm 139:1-4 NIV)

Since God knows us so intimately and loves us so completely, don't be surprised if He will allow you to remember something from long ago that will lay your questions to rest. Never take your memories for granted. Your Father will guide you into all truth and help you to find perfect peace.

> I dined with Peace
> at a table for two
> in a kitchen filled with calm—
> Her words serene,
> a compress for my mind,
> settled me with mellow balm—
>
> Anxiety knocked,
> and I opened the door—
> I let him in
> I led him through
> the kitchen to the table for two—
> With Peace present,
> there was no space for more—
> I should have made Anxiety leave,
> but instead, I offered him a seat—
> Peace responded, and quietly, subtly left—

I chatted long, hard, and heavy
with this newly-welcomed guest
until tension thick filled the room—
I finally bid him go, slammed the door,
sat down at my place,
and caught the eye of Peace
looking my way from the other room—
She stood in the doorway
I asked her to return—
She settled again,
and the fresh breeze of calm returned—
— Curt Dalaba ©2019

I don't want to dwell on anxious thoughts. It's a waste of time. Instead, I want to lift my eyes toward Jesus, the Prince of Peace, and become aware of His presence, allowing myself to find contentment with Him. When a happy memory enters my mind, I want to savor the glimpse I've been given to an event long ago that had once brought me joy. I don't want to take it for granted but see it as the gift from God that it is and lift my voice in thankful worship. As I surrender my disappointment and choose to trust God instead, peace floods my soul and joy soon follows.

> "I lift up my eyes to the mountains—where does my help come from? My help comes from the LORD, the Maker of heaven and earth. He will not let your foot slip—he who watches over you will not slumber; indeed, he who watches over Israel will neither slumber nor sleep. The LORD watches over you—the LORD is your shade at your right hand; the sun will not harm you by day, nor the moon by night. The LORD will keep you from all harm—he will watch over your life; the LORD will watch over your coming and going both now and forevermore." (Psalm 121 NIV)

Although Curt had to go, God is still with me. He is the same today as He always has been. He has not abandoned me to face my grief alone. "The LORD is close to the brokenhearted and saves those who are crushed in spirit." (Psalm 34:18 NIV) In His infinite wisdom, He allowed me to face grief. But He's promised to stay beside me, hold my hand, and walk through it with me. I choose to trust Him and depend on Him.

CHAPTER TWENTY-FOUR

Love Never Ends

Death cannot destroy love. Absence does not blow out its flame. Love continues to burn brightly for the ones we loved and lost. "Place me like a seal over your heart, like a seal on your arm; for love is as strong as death, its jealousy unyielding as the grave … It burns like blazing fire, like a mighty flame. Many waters cannot quench love; rivers cannot sweep it away. If one were to give all the wealth of one's house for love, it would be utterly scorned." (Song of Solomon 8:6–7 NIV)

Somehow, it's reassuring to know that love continues in our hearts. We don't forget our loved ones, nor do we stop loving them. Is it because we—that is, our souls—are eternal beings, so we have the ability to love forever? Not even death can kill love. The reason it hurts so much is because we loved so deeply, and we were loved in return.

How reassuring it is to know that our loved ones are not gone from our sight forever. If they are with God and we are serving God faithfully, our love for each other will never end. Jesus gave us a wonderful promise of eternal life in John 3:16 NIV, "For God so loved the world that he gave his one and only Son, that whoever believes in him shall not perish but have eternal life."

In the meantime, however, I continue to feel the sting of our separation. It hurts. Adjusting to being single again is hard. I'm slowly becoming accustomed to my new life, but I wish I didn't need to.

I came across the following entry in my journal from only a few months ago. I debated long and hard if I should share it in such a public way, but maybe by reading it you will find comfort to know that although time does heal, it does not dim the love we shared.

Dear Curt,

Today is your second birthday in heaven. My love and my longing for you is as strong as ever. As much as I've learned to be independent, I'd give it all up in a moment if I could have you back. I'd willingly rejoin in partnership with you.

Today I forced myself to face another "first". I'm sitting at Sleepy Hollow State Park under a tree on a beach blanket. I couldn't bring myself to come here before now.

I wanted to sit on the bench we had shared two years ago after you hobbled on your crutches to that spot. I can see the dock where I had pushed you in your wheelchair only a couple of weeks later.

The bench was occupied today, and I'm not sure if I'll walk onto the dock. There are several people on it today. Actually, there are people all around me—in the water, on the beach, under shade trees, and at the picnic pavilions.

I hear laughter, conversations, and children shouting and screaming as they splash in the lake. Nobody seems to notice the woman sitting under a lone tree, writing in her journal as her heart bleeds onto the page.

How many times did we walk here? I don't remember. But those were sweet times of sharing our hearts with each other. Your companionship and God's presence were enough. I felt complete with you beside me.

Today, there's a strong breeze to help cool the hot day. Leaves rustle in the trees and birds chirp on the ground as they scavenge for food picnickers accidentally dropped. Life around me continues as it always has. Surely, I'm not the only one here today trying to heal a broken heart. Only God knows what each person has encountered. He knows the burdens they carry. He knows the triumphs and the joys too.

There are probably over one hundred people all around me. I feel insignificant and unseen. When you were beside me, I was never invisible. You saw me. What a wonderful friendship we had—lovers who shared life together. We listened and encouraged each other. It felt natural, never awkward or forced. We were one.

Now, if I want someone to listen to me, I must interrupt their day with a call, a text, or an email. With you, there were no interruptions. We were in continual communion even while apart. Your life was my life, and my life was yours. Interruptions were nonexistent between us. We were always there for each other.

When I lost that closeness with you, I called out

to the Lord. I found Him willing and able to fill all that I'd lost with His presence and comfort. Whenever I reach out to Him, He's always ready to listen. The only time I lose that closeness is when I get distracted by life. Oh, to remember to pray without ceasing.

Curt, I still remember the things you said and taught me. Your words still resonate in my mind and heart. Your life is a legacy I and many others will never forget.

Your children and grandchildren miss you so much. Just last week, Brayden (would you believe he's five now) and I looked at some old videos. We watched videos of you too. Brayden said, "I wish Opa didn't have to go." Oh, how well I understand how he feels.

As much as I long to be with you, I know my work here isn't done. But I will join you one day. By the grace of God and His constant love, guidance, and strength, when my time here is finished, I will see you again. We will be closer than ever before.

My love for you will continue throughout all eternity.

The only thing that has been able to lift my spirit has been to turn my eyes toward Jesus and cling to His promises. He is my hope.

Death isn't the only grief people have to deal with. There are many things in life that can cause deep grief, but no matter what the cause of our grief, God can help.

I'm reminded of a story Curt shared with me about his landlady in Germany. Before I met Curt, he was on a short-term mission's trip in Germany. His landlady, Annelis, lived through World War II and explained what it had been like. She had worked in a hospital, and one day while at work, her city was bombed, including the hospital. When the noise finally settled down, she returned to her duties and began to walk from one ward to the next. When she opened a door at the end of a hallway, she came to a sudden stop. There was nothing there but rubble. The rest of the building was gone.

After a long shift and the stress of wartime anxiety and grief, Annelis felt as though she had reached the end of her ability to cope. The claws of despair dug deep into her soul as she reached her neighborhood which hadn't been spared. As she walked into her home, it all seemed surreal, like a nightmare from which you couldn't wake up. Was she losing her mind?

This is the poem Curt penned about Annelis and the gift God gave her at the lowest moment of her life:

> The neighborhood is ablaze
> as she returns from the hospital.
> She is distraught.
> Her own house is hit
> but not in flames
> like the next-door neighbor's.
>
> She cries out to God,
> "Help me, or I'll go insane!"
> She goes to the living room
> window and looks to the street
> below and sees a grand piano
> in the middle of the street.
>
> In a flash she bounds down
> the stairs into the street.
> Concert pianist that she was,
> she began wildly to play
> Beethoven, and her stress
> poured out her fingertips.
> — Curt Dalaba ©2019

Annelis had told Curt how that piano, in the middle of the street of all places, ended up being a gift from God to help her make it through that day. I imagine the memory of that moment helped her through the rest of the war too. A reminder that God saw her. He allowed an undamaged piano to be placed on the street outside her living room window in the middle of a war! Imagine that. How much God must have loved Annelis, and how aware he was of her deepest need.

When I'm tempted to become fearful about what the future might hold, I remind myself that I chose to trust God. Fixing my gaze on Him causes the problems and heartaches of this life to diminish in size. God is in control, He loves us, and He continues to care for us. His plans are for our eternal good.

"Do not be afraid or discouraged, for the Lord will personally go ahead of you. He will be with you; he will neither fail you nor abandon you." (Deuteronomy 31:8 NLT)

CHAPTER TWENTY-FIVE

What Grief Has Taught Me

As I write this last chapter, it's been two years, three months, and seven days since I lost Curt. I want to share some observations that I hope will help you on your journey:

1. I'm in the healing process, but I'm also still grieving. It seems grief becomes stranger and more unpredictable as the months and years go by. I can't cry like I used to, but I still miss my husband, some days more than others. There are mornings when I still dread facing another

day without him, and then there are mornings when I'm ready to get going with my day, and I don't consciously consider my loss. Living without Curt has become such a part of the fabric of who I am now. Grief or loss weaves its way in and out of my day all day long. It's part of who I am. I don't have to think about Curt to miss him; I just miss him. I don't have to try to remember him; he's never far from my thoughts. I'm living my life without him now, but he's always there. Not physically or even in a ghost-like manner. But his theology, his beliefs, his teachings, his opinions, his deep convictions, his love, his encouragement —all the things I learned from him— those are with me always. Sometimes even his humor.

2. Grief is a lonely experience. You can't compare one person's grief with another person's grief. Someone said, the worst grief is your own grief. That's true. Even if two people lose their spouse and both couples had been married for the same amount of time, their grief might be very different from each other. If one lost her husband after five years of marriage and another after sixty-five years of marriage, is one of them facing greater heartache? Do we need to know the answer to that question? Who can say? Does it hurt more to lose a child than a husband? Who

knows? Each person and situation is so different. Don't compare. They are both grieving. Grief is awful and it's painful, so allow each person to feel their loss without comparison and look for ways to give comfort.

3.   Keep striving to move forward. Resist getting stuck in grief and wallowing in it. Be honest with yourself about this. If you are having a good day, allow yourself to enjoy it. If you are having a wave of grief, then it's okay to cry, talk to God, talk to a close friend who is willing to listen, and allow yourself to feel the pain. Only God can truly comfort you and help free you from the terrible sadness that grief has brought into your life. Only God can heal a broken heart. So we look to Him and join our voices with the psalmist, "My eyes are ever on the LORD, for only he will release my feet from the snare. Turn to me and be gracious to me, for I am lonely and afflicted. Relieve the troubles of my heart and free me from my anguish." (Psalm 25:15–17 NIV) Allow yourself to grieve, but also allow yourself to heal.

4.   Remember that one day your life will also come to an end. How do you want to be remembered? Strive every day to leave behind a beautiful legacy that future generations will want to follow. "Teach us

to number our days, that we may gain a heart of wisdom. Satisfy us in the morning with your unfailing love, that we may sing for joy and be glad all our days." (Psalm 90:12&14 NIV)

We had to bury our loved ones. But let's allow the legacy they left behind to continue through our lives. Let's love and do good deeds. Let's bring laughter and joy. Let's show kindness and care deeply. Let's comfort, listen, and try to understand. Let's make plans and keep on living. Let's remind each other that life is worth living because of the joy that is still to come.

This life is a vapor and will soon pass, and then comes eternity, so grieve with hope and allow God to shine His light into the darkness of your grief.

You light a lamp for me.
The LORD, my God, lights up my darkness.
(Psalm 18:28 NLT)

Forever in my heart.

Can't wait to see you again.

Acknowledgments

• First and foremost, I thank my Heavenly Father for walking through this grief journey with me, never leaving my side. He understood my brokenness, disappointment, longing, and grief. He answered my questions and magnified His presence in my life, giving me greater understanding of His character. All glory be to Him alone!

• I am so thankful for my daughter, Amanda, who stayed with me for one month after I lost Curt. (Thank you Alireza, my loving son-in-law, for sharing Amanda and Leila with me.) Amanda and I cried together as we felt the sting of death—the empty chair at the table, the vacant home office, the Bibles Curt would never read again. Her presence helped me through early grief. Although hundreds of miles separated us all too soon, her daily phone calls, sweet words of encouragement, compassion, and sharing in each other's heartache, were precious to me. I see a lot of her dad in her thought process and how deep her understanding of others is. Her precious Leila has brought much laughter during those times when joy was almost impossible to find. Amanda's writing and editing skills were a great resource and encouragement in my writing process.

• I am so thankful for my son, Brendon. A chip off the old block—so much like his dad in the things that really matter. The same hardworking man of integrity and faithfulness to God and to his family. He grabbed the baton that was passed to him and shouldered the responsibility of caring for a widowed mother from the moment his dad took his last breath. He has helped me in many emotional and practical ways. Brendon, my loving daughter-in-law, Kelsey, and their energetic and fun-loving boys have helped to fill my life and lift the loneliness. How wonderful that they live near me. I so appreciate Brendon's understanding of technology and helpful guidance and assistance in the things that would have overwhelmed me. He made my necessary transition to widowhood easier in many ways.

• I am so thankful that I did not lose Curt's parents the day I lost Curt. They continued to see me as their daughter. They linked arms with me on this journey we share. Our many phone calls and text messages were heartwarming, comforting, and filled with wisdom.

• I am so grateful to my mom and dad. Although my dad has passed away now too, he was there after Curt died. I saw him grieve for the son (because that's how he saw Curt) and pastor he dearly loved. My sweet mom often sat beside me or went for long walks with me so I could talk. She seemed to instinctively know when to give me space and when to come near.

• I'm so thankful for my sister, Margo, who called me and prayed diligently during the cancer battle, sending encouragement through songs and Scripture verses. Although we live far apart, she came to visit and stayed for long periods of time after my loss, helping me pack up Curt's office. We cried and laughed together as we shared memories. Thanks, Robert, for sharing her with me.

• I am so blessed to have a loving and caring brother,

Oz, who helped me by lending his strength in caring for Curt when he had difficulty walking. Oz loved Curt like a brother—the brother he never had—and Curt felt the same. My brother's heart broke the day we lost Curt. Since then, Oz has helped me with many practical things around my house. I so appreciate him.

• I'm thankful for my sister-in-law, Bonnie. Her calls gave me hope because she had walked her own grief journey a few years prior. She listened with great sensitivity that soothed my broken heart. I sensed she understood how I felt.

• Thank you to Greg and Sandie Mundis, who provided me with a stimulating writing project during my grief journey. I'm sure God directed this; there is no other explanation. Sandie became so much more than a colleague. She became my confidante, encourager, and precious friend. I believe God ordained every aspect of leading us together. Their book, *Patient #1*, is worth reading, especially if you're facing a spiritual, emotional, or physical battle.

• Thank you to my dear friends, Pat Brown, Carolyn McElroy, and Becky Wagner, for proofreading my manuscript. You are such a great encouragement, and I appreciate your careful eye for detail, your skill, and your honest input.

• Thank you to my very capable editor, Cristel Phelps. I have so enjoyed our meals together. You are a fount of wisdom when it comes to writing, editing, and publishing. How blessed I am that our paths have crossed. Thank you for helping me make my writing even better.

• I wish I could individually thank each person who has

blessed me on this grief journey. There are so many! Allow me to say a great, big, collective "thank you" to all my family, friends, acquaintances, and readers who prayed for me and sent words of encouragement, songs, Bible verses, poems, and cards. My family and I sensed the prayer support, and our Loving Father was faithful to answer your prayers.

With deepest appreciation,
Anneliese Dalaba

Other Books by this Author

The Arranged Marriage Series is captivating and heart-warming. These are historical Christian romance novels in the Regency England period.

Reluctant to Wed: Two strangers. Opposing dreams. Sparks fly as fears, lies, attraction, and love collide in this arranged marriage.

Emma agrees to an arranged marriage, secretly hoping and praying they will fall in love. She travels from America to England to meet her grandfather, who arranges a marriage between her and the Earl of Devonport. Now she must learn to conform to the dictates of British high society.

The Marriage Maneuver: A masterful deception places two strangers in an arranged marriage neither anticipated nor desired.

Lady Selina Kendall, daughter of a viscount, was given away to her aunt and uncle at a rather young age. She has never understood why she was forced to leave her parents' home while her siblings were allowed to stay. Selina longs for the day she can return to her family.

When she is finally ready to be presented to society, the long-awaited letter from her parents arrives. But when Selina returns home, instead of being warmly embraced, she discovers her parents were ridding themselves of her again. This time, they've arranged a marriage.

***Ties That Bind*:** He needs a wife. She loves another. Forced to marry, will their faith and vows keep them together when others try to tear them apart?

Determined never to marry, Kitty Haddington chooses to assist her father in his parish. After visiting an elderly parishioner outside of town, Kitty is caught in a snowstorm and injured while attempting to return home. Her infuriating rescuer seems oblivious to their precarious situation. If they remain together for too long, marriage might be the only way to salvage her reputation. Should he deem it necessary to marry her, the unfortunate man would find himself in a loveless union, for her heart would always belong to another.

Made in the USA
Monee, IL
27 June 2023

37792881R00102